The House We Live In

Based on—
First Book in Physiology and Hygiene

by
John Harvey Kellogg, M.D.

Revised and edited by
Leonard Brazille, Arnet Mathers,
Cinthia Lowe, and Jeff Reich

LMN Publishing International

The House We Live In
Based on—
First Book in Physiology and Hygiene

ISBN 0-9665786-0-0

LMN Publishing International, Inc.
HC04, Box 94C
St. Maries, Idaho, 83861

For additional copies of this book, or
for a list of other available materials,
write to the above address or call:
1-800-245-1844

Contents

To the Teacher

This book is intended for children. The special objects which the author has aimed to accomplish in the preparation of the work have been:

1. To present as fully as possible and proper in a work of this character a statement of the laws of healthful living, giving such special prominence to the subject of stimulants and narcotics as its recognized importance and the recent laws relating to the study of this branch of hygiene demand.

2. To present in a simple manner such anatomical and physiological facts as shall give the child a good fundamental knowledge of the structure and functions of the human body.

3. To present each topic in such clear and simple language as to enable the pupil to comprehend the subject matter with little aid from the teacher; and to observe in the manner of presentation the principle that the things to be studied should be placed before the mind of the child before they are named. A natural and logical order has been observed in the sequence of topics. Technical terms have been used very sparingly, and only in their natural order, and are then fully explained and their pronunciation indicated, so that it is not thought necessary to append a glossary.

4. To present the subjects of physiology and hygiene in the light of the most recent authentic researches in these branches of science, and to avoid the numerous errors which have for many years been current in the school literature of these subjects.

There is no subject in the presentation of which object-teaching may be employed with greater facility and profit than in teaching physiology, and none which may be more advantageously impressed upon the student's mind by means of simple experimentation than the subject of hygiene. Every teacher who uses this book is urgently requested to supplement each lesson by the use of object-teaching or experiments. A great number of simple experiments illustrative of both physiology and hygiene may be readily arranged. Many little experiments are suggested in the text, which should invariably be made before the class, each member of which should also be encouraged to repeat them at home.

It is also most desirable that the teacher should have the aid of suitable charts and models.

In conclusion, the author would acknowledge his indebtedness for a large number of useful suggestions and criticisms to several medical friends and experienced teachers, and especially to Professor Henry Sewall, of the University of Michigan, for criticisms of the portions of the work relating to physiology.

J. H. KELLOGG, 1887

Chapter 1

The House We Live In

1. Object of this Book—The object of this book is to tell the little boys and girls who read it about a wonderful house. You have all seen some very beautiful houses. Perhaps they were made of brick or stone, with fine porches, having around them tall shade trees, smooth lawns, pretty flower—beds, walks, and sparkling fountains.

2. Perhaps some of you live in such a house, or have visited some friend who does. If so, you know that the inside of the house is even more beautiful than the outside. There are elegant chairs and sofas in the rooms, rich carpets and rugs on the floors, fine mirrors and beautiful pictures upon the walls—everything one could wish to have in a house. Do you not think such a house a nice one to live in?

3. The Body is Like a House—Each of us has a house of his own which is far more wonderful and more curious than the grandest palace ever built. It is not a very large house. It has just room enough in it for one person. This house, which belongs to each one of us, is called the body.

4. What is a Machine?—Do you know what a machine is? Men make machines to help them work and to do many useful things. A wheelbarrow or a wagon is a machine to carry loads. A sewing-machine helps to make garments for us to wear. Clocks and watches are machines for keeping time.

5. A Machine has Different Parts—A wheelbarrow has a box in which to carry things, two handles to hold by, and a wheel for rolling it along. Some machines, like wheelbarrows and wagons, have but few parts, and it is very easy for us to learn how they work. But there are other machines, like watches and sewing-machines, which have many different parts, and it is more difficult to learn all about them and what they do.

6. The Body is Like a Machine—In some ways the body is more like a machine than like a house. It has many different parts which are made to do a great many different kinds of work. We see with our eyes, hear with our ears, walk with our legs and feet, and do a great many things with our hands. If you have ever seen the inside of a watch or a clock you know how many curious little wheels it has. And yet a watch or a clock can do but one thing, and that is to tell us the time of day. The body has a great many more parts than a watch has and for this reason the body can do many more things than a watch can do. It is more difficult, too, to learn about the body than about a watch.

7. If we want to know all about a machine and how it works, we must study all its different parts and learn how they are put together, and what each part does. Then, if we want the machine to work well and to last a long time, we must know how to use it and how to take proper care of it. Do you think your watch would keep the time well if you should neglect to wind it, or if you should break any of its wheels?

8. It is just the same with the human machine which we call the body. We must learn its parts, and what they are for, how they are made, how they are put together, and how they work. Then we must learn how to take proper care of the body, so that its parts will be able to work well and last a long time.

9. Each part of the body which is made to do some special kind of work is called an organ. The eye, the ear, the nose, a hand, an arm, any part of the body that does something, is an organ.

10. The study of the various parts of the body and how they are put together is *anatomy* (a-nat'-o-my). The study of what each part of the body does is *physiology* (phys-i-ol'-o-gy). The study of how to take care of the body is *hygiene* (hy-jeen).

SUMMARY

1. The body is something like a house. It has an outside and an inside; it has hollow places inside of it, and there are many wonderful things in them.

2. They body is also like a wonderful machine.

3. It is necessary to take good care of the body in order to keep it well and useful, just as we would take good care of a machine to keep it from wearing out too soon.

4. The body has many different parts, called organs, each of which has some particular work to do.

5. In learning about the body, we have to study anatomy, physiology, and hygiene.

6. The study of the various parts of the body, how they are formed and joined together, is anatomy. Physiology tells us what the body does, hygiene tells us how to take care of it.

Chapter 2

A General View of the Body

1. Parts of the Body—What do we call the main part of a tree? The trunk, you say. The main part of the body is also called its *trunk*. There are two arms and two legs growing out of the human trunk. The branches of a tree we call *limbs*, and so we speak of the arms and legs as limbs. We sometimes call the arms the *upper extremities*, and the legs the *lower extremities*. At the top of the trunk is the head.

2. Names of the Parts—Now let us look more closely at these different parts. As we speak the name of each part, let each one touch that part of himself which is named. We will begin with the head. The chief parts of the head are the *skull* and the *face*. The *forehead*, the *temples*, the *cheeks*, the *eyes*, the *ears*, the *nose*, the *mouth*, and the *chin* are parts of the face.

3. The chief parts of the trunk are the *chest*, the *abdomen* (ab'-do-men), and the *backbone*. The head is joined to the trunk by the *neck*.

4. Each arm has a *shoulder*, *upper arm*, *forearm*, *wrist*, and *hand*. The *fingers* are a part of the hand.

5. Each leg has a *hip, thigh, lower leg, ankle,* and *foot*. The *toes* are a part of the foot.

6. Our hands and face and the whole body are covered with something as soft and smooth as the finest silk. It is the skin. What is it that grows from the skin on the head? and what at the ends of the fingers and the toes? We shall learn more about the skin, the hair, and the nails in another lesson.

7. The body has two sides, the right side and the left side, which are alike. We have two eyes, two ears, two arms, etc. We have but one nose, one mouth, and one chin, but each of these organs has two halves, which are just alike.

SUMMARY

1. The body has a head and trunk, two arms, and two legs.

2. The parts of the head are the skull and face. The forehead, temples, cheeks, eyes, ears, nose, mouth and chin are parts of the face.

3. The parts of the trunk are the chest, abdomen, and backbone. The neck joins the head and trunk.

4. Each arm has a shoulder, upper arm, forearm, wrist, and hand. The fingers belong to the hand.

5. Each leg has a hip, thigh, lower leg, ankle, and foot. The toes belong to the foot.

6. The whole body is covered by the skin.

7. The two sides of the body are alike.

Chapter 3

The Inside of the Body

1. Thus far we have taken only a brief look at the outside of the body, and we have found out very little about its many wonderful parts. Very likely you want to ask a great many questions, such as, How does the inside of the body look? What is in the skull? What is in the chest? What is in the abdomen? Why do we eat and drink? Why do we become hungry and thirsty? What makes us tired and sleepy? How do we keep warm? Why do we breathe? How do we grow? How do we move about? How do we talk, laugh, and sing? How do we see, hear, feel, taste, and smell? How do we remember, think, and reason? All these, and a great many more interesting questions, you will find answered in the following lessons, if you study each one well.

2. When we study the inside of the body, we begin to understand how wonderfully we are made. We cannot all see the inside of the body, and it is not necessary that we should do so. Many learned men have spent their whole lives in seeking to find out all about our bodies and the bodies of various animals.

3. The Bones—If you take hold of your arm, it seems soft on the outside; and if you press upon it, you will feel something hard inside. The soft part is called *flesh*. The hard part is called *bone*. If you wish, you can easily get one of the bones of an animal at the butcher's shop, or you may find some out in the wild.

4. The Skeleton—All the bones of an animal, when placed properly together, have nearly the shape of the body, and are called the *skeleton* (skel'-e-ton). The skeleton forms the framework of the body, just as the heavy timbers of a house form its framework. It supports all the parts.

5. The Skull—The bony part of the head is called the *skull*. In the skull is a hollow place or chamber. You know that a bank often has a strongroom or a safe in which is kept money, important papers, and other valuable things. The chamber in the skull is the strongroom, or the safe, of the body. It has strong, tough walls of bone, and contains the brain. The brain is the most important and also the most tender and delicate organ in the whole body. This is why it is so carefully guarded from injury.

6. The Backbone—The framework of the back is called the *backbone*. This is not a single bone, but a row of bones arranged one above another. Each bone has a hole through it, about as large as one of your fingers. A large branch from the brain, called the *spinal cord*, runs down through the middle of the backbone, so that the separate bones look as if they were strung on the spinal cord, like beads on a string.

7. The Trunk—The trunk of the body, like the skull, is hollow. Its walls are formed partly by the backbone and the ribs and partly by flesh. A fleshy wall divides the hollow of the trunk into two parts, an upper chamber called the chest, and a lower called the *abdomen*.

8. The Lungs and Heart—The chest contains a pair of organs called the *lungs*, with which we breathe. It also contains something which we can feel beating at the left side. This is the *heart*. The heart lies between the two lungs, and a little to the left side.

9. The Stomach and Liver—In the abdomen are some very wonderful organs that do different kinds of work for the body. Among them are the *stomach*, the *bowels*, and the *liver*. There are, also, other organs whose names we shall learn when we come to study them.

10. Care of the Body—We have only begun to study the beautiful house in which we live, and yet have we not learned enough to show us how great and wise is the Creator who made us and all the wonderful machinery within our bodies? If someone should give you a beautiful present, would you treat it carelessly and spoil it, or would you take good care of it and keep it nice as long as possible? Ought we not to take such care of our bodies as to keep them in that perfect and beautiful condition in which our kind and good Creator gave them to us?

SUMMARY

1. The body has a framework called the skeleton.

2. The skeleton is made up of many different parts, each of which is called a bone.

3. The bones are covered by the flesh.

4. The bones of the head form the skull, which is hollow and contains the brain.

5. A row of bones arranged in the back, one above another, forms the backbone. The backbone has a canal running through it lengthwise, in which lies the spinal cord.

6. The trunk is hollow and has two chambers, one called the cavity of the chest, and the other the cavity of the abdomen.

7. The chest contains the two lungs and the heart.

8. The abdomen contains the stomach, liver, and many other very important organs.

9. Is it not our duty to take good care of our bodies as we would of some nice present from a friend?

Chapter 4

Our Foods

1. We all know very well that if we do not eat we shall rapidly lose in weight and become very weak and feeble. Did you ever think how much one eats in the course of a lifetime? Let's see if we can figure it out. How much do you suppose a boy eats in a day? Let us say two pounds. How much does he eat in a year? There are three hundred and sixty-five days in a year; 365 multiplied by 2 equals 730. So a boy eats a good many times his own weight in a year. How much would a person eat in fifty years?

2. Our bodies are composed of what we eat. If we eat bad food, our bodies will be made out of poor material and will not be able to do their work well. So you see how important it is to learn something about our foods. We ought to know what things are good for us to eat, and what will do us harm.

3. **Foods and Poisons**—Foods are those substances which nourish the body and keep it in good working order.

4. Our foods are obtained from both animals and plants. All food really comes from plants, for even those animals which some people use as food themselves live upon the vegetables which they eat. For example, the ox and the cow eat grass and furnish people with beef and milk. Chickens eat corn and other grains, and supply eggs and meat also.

5. The principal animal foods are milk, cheese, eggs, and the different kinds of flesh—beef, mutton, pork, fish, fowl, and wild game.

We obtain a great many more kinds of food from plants than from animals. Most plant foods are included in three classes—*fruits*, *grains*, and *vegetables*.

6. *Fruits* are the fleshy parts of plants which contain the seeds. Our most common fruits are apples, pears, peaches, plums, cherries, and various kinds of nuts. Perhaps you know of some other kinds of fruit besides those mentioned. Your teacher will tell you that tomatoes, watermelons, and pumpkins are really fruits, though they are not generally so called.

7. The seeds of grass-like plants are known as grains, of which we have wheat, rye, barley, corn, and rice. There are a few seeds that grow in pods, such as peas and beans, which somewhat resemble grains.

8. We eat the leaves, stems, or roots of some plants, as cabbages, celery, turnips, and potatoes. Foods of this kind are called *vegetables*.

9. There are other things, which, if we eat or drink them, will make us sick or otherwise do us harm. These are called *poisons*. Only such food as is pure and free from poisons is good or safe for us to use.

10. **Narcotics and Stimulants**—There are a number of substances known as narcotics and stimulants, which, from their effects upon the body, may be classed as poisons. Tobacco, opium, alcohol, and cocaine are included in this class. Death has been caused by taking these poisonous drugs. We shall learn more of the effects of tobacco and alcohol in future lessons.

SUMMARY

1. Our bodies are made of what we eat.

2. Things which will help us to grow strong and well, if we eat them, are foods.

3. We get foods from plants and animals.

4. There are several kinds of animal foods, and three classes of plant foods—fruits, grains, and vegetables.

5. Things which make us sick when we eat them are poisons.

Chapter 5

Unhealthful Foods

1. Many people eat things which are not good for them. Some people do not stop to think whether what they eat is good for them or likely to do them harm. Sometimes, without knowing it, we eat things which are harmful to us. Do you not think that we should try to learn what is good to eat and what is not good, and then be very careful not to eat anything which is likely to do us harm?

2. Diseased Foods— When a person is sick, he is said to be diseased. Animals are sometimes sick or diseased. Vegetables are also sometimes diseased. Animals and vegetables that are diseased are not good for food. Dishonest men, however, sometimes sell them to those who do not know that they are unfit to be eaten.

3. Pork, the flesh of the hog, is more likely to be diseased than any other kind of animal food.

4. Beef and mutton may be diseased also. Sheep and cattle are sometimes sick of diseases very much like those which human beings have. Meat which is pale, yellowish, or of a dark red color, is unhealthful, and should not be eaten. Meat should never be eaten raw. If it is going

Tobacco Plant

to be eaten, it should always be well cooked.

5. Unripe Foods—Most vegetable foods are unfit to be eaten when green or unripe, especially if uncooked. Sometimes persons are made very sick indeed by eating such articles as green apples or unripe peaches.

6. Stale or Decayed Foods—Food which has been allowed to stand until it is spoiled, or has become *stale*, *musty*, or *moldy*, such as moldy bread or fruit, or tainted meat, is unfit to be eaten, and is often a cause of sickness. Canned fish or other meats spoil very quickly after the cans are opened.

7. Condiments—These are substances which are added to our food for the purpose of giving to it special flavors. Condiments are not foods, because they do not nourish the body in any way, and are not necessary to preserve it in health.

8. The most common condiments are mustard, pepper, pepper sauce, ginger, cayenne pepper, and spices. All these substances are irritating. If we put mustard upon the skin, it will make the skin red, and in a little time will raise a blister. If we happen to get a little pepper in the eye, it makes it become irritated and become very red and inflamed. When we take these things into the stomach, they cause the stomach to irritated, and its lining membrane becomes red just as the skin or the eye does.

9. Nature has put into our foods very nice flavors to make us enjoy eating them. Condiments are likely to do us great harm, and hence it is far better not to use them.

10. **Tobacco**—Most of you know that tobacco is obtained from a plant which has long, broad leaves. These leaves are dried and then rolled up into cigars, ground into snuff, shredded into cigarettes, or prepared for chewing.

11. Tobacco has a smarting, sickening taste. Do you think it would be good to eat? Why not?

12. You know that tobacco makes people sick when they first begin to use it. This is because it contains a very deadly poison called *nicotine*.

13. If you give tobacco to a cat or a dog, it will become very sick. A boy once gave a piece of tobacco to a monkey, which swallowed it not knowing what a bad thing it was. The monkey soon became sick and died.

14. Many learned doctors have noticed the effects which come from using tobacco, and they all say it does great harm to boys and girls, that it makes them puny and weak, and prevents their growing up into strong and useful men. If tobacco is not good for monkeys, do you think it could be good for boys and girls? If it is not good for boys and girls, do you think it can be good for men and women? Certainly you will say, No.

SUMMARY

1. Both animals and plants are sometimes diseased. Flesh obtained from sick or diseased animals is unfit for food.

2. Unripe, stale, and moldy foods are unfit to be eaten and may cause illness.

3. Foods are sometimes spoiled by having things mixed with them which are not food, or which are poisonous.

4. Tobacco, while not actually eaten, is thought by some persons to be a food, but it is not. It is a poison, and injures all who use it.

5. Boys who use tobacco do not grow strong in body and mind.

Chapter 6

Our Drinks

1. Water is the drink that God originally designed for man. It is the only substance which will satisfy thirst. All other fluids which we drink consist mostly of water. Thus, lemonade is lemon juice and water. Milk is chiefly water. Wine, beer, cider, and such liquids contain alcohol and many other things, mixed with water.

2. **Why We Need Water**—If we should wet a sponge and lay it away, it would become dry in a few hours, as the water would evaporate into the air. Our bodies are losing water all the time, and we need to drink to keep ourselves from drying up.

3. Water is also very necessary for other purposes. It softens our food, so that we can chew and swallow it, and helps to carry it around in the body after it has been digested, in a way about which we shall learn in future lessons.

4. Still another use for water is to dissolve and wash out of our bodies, through the sweat of the skin, and in other ways, the waste and worn-out particles which are no longer of any use.

5. **Impure Water**—Most waters have more or less substances dissolved in them. Water which has much lime in it is called hard water. Such water is not so good to drink or for use in cooking as soft water. That water is best which holds no substances in solution. Well water sometimes contains substances which soak into wells from vaults or cesspools. Chemicals or other substances containing impurities which are poured upon the ground soak down out of sight; but these foul substances are not destroyed. They remain in the soil, and when the rains come, they are washed down into the well if it is near by. You can see some of the things found in bad water in the illustration.

6. It is best not to drink iced water when the body is heated, or during meals. If it is necessary to drink very cold water, the bad effects may be avoided by sipping it very slowly.

7. **Tea and Coffee**—Many people drink tea or coffee at their meals, and some persons think that

A DROP OF IMPURE WATER MAGNIFIED

these drinks are useful foods; but they really have little or no value as foods. Both tea and coffee contain a poison call *caffeine* (caf-feen'), which, when separated in a pure form, is very poisonous, so that a small quantity is enough to kill a cat or a dog. This poison often does much harm to those who drink tea or coffee very strong for any great length of time.

8. **Alcohol** (al' co-hol)—All of you know something about alcohol. Perhaps you have seen it burn in a lamp. It will burn without a lamp, if we light it. It is so clear and colorless that it looks like water. The native American Indians, years ago, used to call it "firewater." Alcohol differs very much from foods. It is not grown like plants, as are fruits and grains; neither is it supplied by nature ready for our use, as are air and water.

FERMENTATION

9. **Fermentation**—When a baker makes bread he puts some yeast in the dough to make it "rise," so the bread will be light. The yeast destroys some of the sugar and starch in the flour and changes it into alcohol and a gas. The gas bubbles up through the dough, and this is what makes the bread light. This is called *fermentation* (fer-men-ta'-tion). The little alcohol which is formed in the bread does no harm, because it is all driven off by the heat when the bread is baked.

10. Any moist substance or liquid which contains sugar will ferment if yeast is added to it, or if it is kept in a warm place. You know that canned fruit sometimes spoils. This is because it ferments. Fermentation is a sort of decay. When the juice of grapes, apples, or other fruit is allowed to stand in a warm place, it "works," or ferments, and thus produces alcohol. Wine is fermented grape juice; hard cider is fermented apple juice.

11. Beer, ale, and similar drinks are made from grains. The grain is first moistened and allowed to sprout. In sprouting, the starch of the grain is changed to sugar. The grain is next dried and ground, and is then boiled with water. The water dissolves the sugar. The sweet liquid thus obtained is separated from the grain, and yeast is added to it. This causes it to ferment, which changes the sugar to alcohol.

Thus we see that the grain does not contain alcohol in the first place, but that it is produced by fermentation.

12. All fermented liquids contain more or less alcohol, mixed with water and a good many other things. Rum, brandy, gin, whiskey, and pure alcohol are made by separating the alcohol from the other substances. This is done by means of a still and is called *distillation*.

13. You can learn how a still separates the alcohol by a little experiment. When a teapot is boiling on the stove and the steam is coming out at the nozzle, hold up to the nozzle a common drinking-glass filled with iced water, first taking care to wipe the outside of the glass perfectly dry. Little drops of water will soon gather upon the side of the glass. If you touch these to the tongue you will observe that they taste of the tea. It is because a little of the tea has escaped with the steam and condensed upon the glass. This is distillation.

14. If the teapot had contained wine, or beer, or hard cider, the distilled water would have contained alcohol instead of tea. By distilling the liquid several times the alcohol may be obtained almost pure.

15. **Alcohol Kills Plants**—Strong alcohol has a deadly effect upon all living things. If you should pour alcohol upon a plant it would die very soon.

16. A man once made a cruel experiment. He put some minnows into a jar of water and then poured in a few teaspoonfuls of alcohol. The minnows tried very hard to get out, but they

could not, and in a little while they were all dead, poisoned by the alcohol. A Frenchman once gave alcohol to some pigs with their food. They soon became sick and died.

17. Alcohol Not a Food—There are some people who imagine that alcohol is good for food because it is made from fruits and grains which are good for food. This is a serious mistake. A person can live on the fruits or grains from which alcohol is made, but no one would attempt to live upon alcohol. If he did, he would soon starve to death. In fact, men have often died in consequence of trying to use whiskey in place of food.

18. We should remember, also, that people do not take alcohol as a food, but for certain effects which it produces, which are not those of a food, but of a poison.

19. Many people who would not drink strong or distilled liquors, think that they will suffer no harm if they use only wine, beer, or cider. This is a great mistake. These liquids contain alcohol, as do all fermented drinks. A person will become drunk or intoxicated by drinking wine, beer, or cider—only a larger quantity is required to produce the same effect as rum or whiskey.

20. Another very serious thing to be thought of is that if a person forms the habit of drinking wine, cider, or other fermented drinks, he becomes so fond of the *effect they produce* that he soon wants some stronger drink, and thus he is led to use whiskey or other strong liquors. On this account it is not safe to use any kind of alcoholic drinks, either fermented or distilled. The only safe plan is to avoid the use of every sort of stimulating or intoxicating drinks.

21. It has been found by observation that those persons who use intoxicating drinks are not so healthy as those who do not use them, and, as a rule, they do not live so long.

DISTILLATION

22. This is found to be true not only of those who use whiskey and other strong liquors, but also of those who use fermented drinks, such as wine and beer. Beer drinkers are much more likely to suffer from disease than those who are strictly temperate. It is often noticed by physicians that when a beer-drinker becomes sick or meets with an accident, he does not recover so readily as one who uses no kind of alcoholic drinks.

23. Alcoholic drinks not only make people unhealthy and shorten their lives, but they are also the cause of much poverty, crime, accidents, and an untold amount of misery.

SUMMARY

1. Water is the only substance that will satisfy thirst.

2. In going through our bodies, water washes out many impurities. Water also softens our food.

3. The purest water is the best. Impure water causes sickness.

4. Good water has no color, taste, or odor.

5. Tea and coffee are not good drinks. They are very injurious to children, and often do older persons much harm.

6. Alcohol is made by fermentation.

7. Pure alcohol and strong liquors are made by distillation.

8. Alcohol is not a food, it is a poison. It kills plants, and is very injurious to animals and human beings.

9. Even the moderate use of alcoholic drinks produces disease and shortens life.

Chapter 7

How We Digest

VENUS FLY-TRAP

1. Have you ever see a Venus fly-trap? This curious plant grows in North Carolina. It is called a flytrap because it has on each of its leaves something like a steel-trap, by means of which it catches flies. You can see one of these traps in the picture. When a fly touches the leaf, the trap shuts up at once, and the poor fly is caught and cannot get away. The harder it tries to escape, the more tightly the trap closes upon it, until after a time it is crushed to death.

2. But we have yet to learn the most curious thing about this strange plant, which seems to act so much like an animal. If we open the leaf after a few days, it will be found that the fly has almost entirely disappeared. The fly has not escaped, but it has been dissolved by a fluid formed inside of the trap, and the plant has absorbed a portion of the fly. In fact, it has really eaten it. The process by which food is dissolved and changed so that it can be absorbed and may nourish the body, is called *digestion* (di-ges'-tion).

3. The Venus's-flytrap has a very simple way of digesting its food. Its remarkable little trap serves it as a mouth to catch and hold its food, and as a stomach to digest it. The arrangement by which our food is digested is much less simple than this. Let us study the different parts by which this wonderful work is done.

4. The Digestive Tube—The most important part of the work of digesting our food is done in a long tube within the body, called the *digestive tube* or *canal.*

5. This tube is twenty-five or thirty feet long in a full-grown man; but it is so coiled up and folded away that it occupies but little space. It begins at the mouth, and ends at the lower part of the trunk. The greater part of it is coiled up in the abdomen.

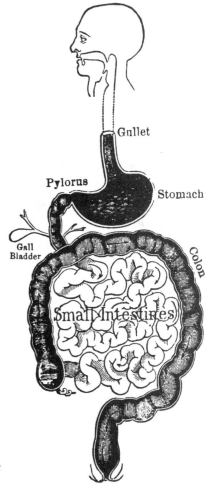

THE DEGESTIVE TUBE

6. The Mouth—The space between the upper and the lower jaw is called the *mouth*. The lips form the front part and the cheeks the sides. At the back part are three openings. One, the upper, leads into the nose. There are two lower openings. One of these leads into the stomach, and the other leads to the lungs. The back part of the mouth joins the two tubes which lead from the mouth to the lungs and the stomach, and is called the *throat*. The mouth contains the *tongue* and the *teeth*.

7. The Teeth—The first teeth, those which come when we are small children, are called *temporary*, or *milk teeth*. We lose these teeth as the jaws get larger and the second, or permanent, teeth take their place. There are twenty teeth in the first set, and thirty-two in the second. Very old persons sometimes have a third set of teeth.

8. The Salivary (sal'-i-vary) **Glands**—There are three pairs of *salivary glands*. They form a fluid called the *saliva* (sa-li'-va). It is this fluid which moistens the mouth at all times. When we eat or taste something which we like, the salivary glands make so much saliva that we sometimes say the mouth waters. One pair of the salivary glands is at the back part of the lower jaw, in front of the ears. The other two pairs of glands are placed at the under side of the mouth. The saliva produced by the salivary glands is sent into the mouth through little tubes called *ducts*.

9. The Gullet—At the back part of the throat begins a narrow

THE TEETH

tube, which passes down to the stomach. This tube is about nine inches long. It is called the *gullet*, *foodpipe*, or *esophagus* (e-soph'-a-gus).

10. The Stomach—At the lower end of the esophagus the digestive tube becomes enlarged, and has a shape somewhat like a pear. This is the *stomach*. In a full-grown person the stomach is sufficiently large to hold about three pints. At each end of the stomach is a narrow opening so arranged that it can be opened or tightly closed, as may be necessary. The upper opening allows the food to pass into the stomach, the lower one allows it to pass out into the intestines. This opening is called the *pylorus* (py-lo'-rus), or gatekeeper, because it closes so as to keep the food in the stomach until it is ready to pass out.

11. In the membrane which lines the stomach there are many little pocket-like glands, in which a fluid called the *gastric juice* is formed. This fluid is one of the most important of all the fluids formed in the digestive canal.

12. The Intestine (intes'-tine)—At the lower end of the stomach the digestive canal becomes narrow again. This narrow portion, called the *intestine*, is about twenty-five feet long in a grown

SALIVARY GLANDS

person. The last few feet of the intestine is larger than the rest and is called the *colon*. This long tube is coiled up and snugly packed away in the cavity of the abdomen. In the membrane lining the intestines are to be found little glands, which make a fluid called *intestinal juice*.

GASTRIC GLAND

13. The Liver—Close up under the ribs, on the right side of the body, is a large brown-colored organ, called the *liver*. The liver is about half as large as the head, and is shaped so as to fit snugly into its corner of the abdomen. The chief business of the liver is to make a fluid called *bile*, which is very necessary for the digestion of our food.

14. The bile is a bitter fluid of a golden-brown color. It is carried to the intestine by means of a little tube or duct, which enters the small intestine a few inches below the stomach. When the bile is made faster than it is needed for immediate use, it is stored up in a little pear-shaped sac called the *gallbladder*, which hangs from the underside of the liver.

15. The liver is a very wonderful organ and does many useful things besides making bile. It aids in various ways in digesting the food, and helps to keep the blood pure by removing from it harmful substances which are formed within the body.

16. The Pancreas (pan'-cre-as)—The *pancreas* is another large and very important gland which is found close to the stomach, lying just behind it in the abdominal cavity. The pancreas forms a fluid called the *pancreatic juice*, which enters the small intestine at nearly the same place as the bile.

17. The Spleen—Close to the pancreas, at the left side of the body, is a dark, roundish organ about the size of the fist, called the *spleen*. It is not known that the spleen has much to do in the work of digestion, but it is so closely connected with the digestive organs that we need to know about it.

18. Please note that there are five important organs of digestion—the mouth, the stomach, the intestines, the pancreas, and the liver.

19. Also observe that there are five digestive fluids—saliva, gastric juice, bile, pancreatic juice, and intestinal juice.

SUMMARY

1. The process of dissolving and changing the food so that it may be absorbed and may nourish the body is digestion.

2. The work of digestion is chiefly done in the digestive tube or canal, which is about thirty feet in length.

3. The mouth contains the teeth and has three pairs of salivary glands connected with it, which make saliva.

4. The gullet leads from the mouth to the stomach.

5. The stomach is pear-shaped and holds about three pints.

6. It has an upper and a lower opening, each of which is guarded by a muscle, which keeps its contents from escaping.

7. The lower opening of the stomach is called the pylorus.

8. The stomach forms the gastric juice.

9. The intestines are about twenty-five feet long. They form the intestinal juice.

10. The liver lies under the ribs of the right side. It is about half as large as the head. It makes bile.

11. When not needed for immediate use, the bile is stored up in a sac called the gallbladder.

12. The pancreas is a gland which lies just back of the stomach. It makes pancreatic juice.

13. The spleen is found near the pancreas.

14. There are five important digestive organs—the mouth, the stomach, the intestines, the liver, and the pancreas.

15. There are five digestive fluids—saliva, gastric juice, intestinal juice, bile, and pancreatic juice.

Chapter 8

Digestion of a Mouthful of Bread

1. Let us suppose that we have eaten a mouthful of bread and can watch it as it goes through all the different processes of digestion.

2. Mastication—First, we chew or masticate the food with the teeth. We use the tongue to move the food from one side of the mouth to the other, and to keep the food between the teeth.

3. Mouth Digestion—While the bread is being chewed, the saliva is mixed with it and acts upon it. The saliva moistens and softens the food, so that it can be easily swallowed and readily acted upon by the other digestive juices. You have noticed that if you chew a bit of hard bread a few minutes it becomes sweet. This is because the saliva changes some of the starch of the food into sugar.

4. After we have chewed the food, we swallow it, and it passes down through the esophagus into the stomach.

5. Stomach Digestion—As soon as the morsel of food enters the stomach, the gastric juice begins to flow out of the little glands in which it is formed. This mingles with the food and digests another portion which the saliva has not acted upon. While this is being done, the stomach keeps working the food much as a baker kneads dough. This is done to mix the gastric juice with the food.

6. After an hour or two the stomach squeezes the food so hard that a little of it, which has been digested by the gastric juice and the saliva, escapes through the lower opening, the pylorus, of which we have already learned. As the action of the stomach continues, more of the digested food escapes, until all that has been properly acted upon has passed out.

7. Intestinal Digestion—We sometimes eat a nut butter with bread, or take some other form of fat in our food. Fats are not acted upon by the saliva or the gastric juice. When food passes out of the stomach into the small intestine, a large quantity of bile is at once poured upon it. This bile has been made beforehand by the liver and stored up in the gallbladder. The bile helps to digest fats, which the saliva and the gastric juice cannot digest.

8. The pancreatic juice does the same kind of work that is done by the saliva, the gastric juice, and the bile. It also finishes up the work done by these fluids. It is one of the most important of all the digestive juices.

9. The intestinal juice digests nearly all the different elements of the food, so that it is well fitted to complete the wonderful process by which the food is made ready to enter the blood and to nourish the body.

10. While the food is being acted upon by the bile, the pancreatic juice, and intestinal juice, it is gradually moved along the intestines. After all those portions of food which can be digested have been softened and dissolved, they are ready to be taken into the blood and distributed through the body.

11. Absorption—If you put a dry sponge into water, it very soon becomes wet by soaking up the water. Indeed, if you only touch a corner of the sponge to the water, the whole sponge will soon become wet. We say that the sponge absorbs the water. It is in a somewhat similar way that the food is taken up or absorbed by the walls of the stomach and intestines. When the food is absorbed, the greater part of it is taken into the blood vessels, of which we shall learn in a future lesson.

12. Liver Digestion—After the food has been absorbed, the most of it is carried to the liver, where the process of digestion is completed. The liver also acts like an inspector to examine the digested food and remove hurtful substances which may be taken with it, such as alcohol, mustard, pepper, and other irritating things.

13. The Thoracic Duct—A portion of the food, especially the digested fats, is absorbed by a portion of the lymphatic vessels called *lacteals*, which empty into a small vessel called the *thoracic duct*. This duct passes upward in front of the spine and empties into a vein near the heart.

14. A Wonderful Creation—As we have studied how our food is digested, we can truly say with the psalmist, "I will praise Thee; for I am fearfully and wonderfully made." Psalm 139:14

SUMMARY

How a mouthful of food is digested:

1. It is first masticated—that is, it is chewed and moistened with saliva.

2. Then it is swallowed, passing through the esophagus to the stomach.

3. There it is acted upon, and a part of it is digested by the gastric juice.

4. It is then passed into the small intestine, where it is acted upon by the bile, the pancreatic fluid, and the intestinal juice.

5. The digested food is then absorbed by the walls of the stomach and intestines.

6. The absorbed food is next passed through the liver, where hurtful substances are removed.

7. A smaller portion is carried through the thoracic duct and emptied into a vein near the heart.

Chapter 9

Bad Habits in Eating

1. Eating Too Fast—A most common fault is eating too fast. When the food is chewed too rapidly and swallowed too quickly it is not properly divided and softened. Such food cannot be easily acted upon by the various digestive juices.

2. Eating Too Much—A person who eats food too rapidly is also very likely to injure himself by eating too much. The digestive organs are able to do well only a certain amount of work. When too much food is eaten, it is not digested as well as it should be. Food which is not well digested will not be as nourishing to the body. Overeating is very common and its results are often seen in the world today.

3. Eating Too Often—Many children make themselves sick by eating too often. It is very harmful to have snacks or to eat at other than the proper mealtimes. The stomach needs time to rest, just as our legs and arms and the other parts of the body do. For the same reason, it is well for us to avoid eating late at night. The stomach needs to sleep with the rest of the body. If one goes to bed with the stomach full of food, the stomach cannot rest, and the work of digestion will go on so slowly that the sleep will likely be disturbed. Such sleep is not refreshing.

4. If we wish to keep our digestive organs in good order, we must take care to eat at regular hours. We ought not to eat when we are very tired. The stomach cannot digest well when we are very much fatigued.

5. Sweet Foods—We ought not to eat too much sugar or sweet foods, as they are likely to sour or ferment in the stomach, and so make us sick. Candies often contain a great many things that are not good for us, which may make us sick. The colors used in candies are not always the most healthful, being made from chemicals. The flavors used in them are oftentimes artificial, made of chemicals that do not build up the body that God has given us.

6. Fatty Foods Hurtful—Too much butter, margarines, fatty meats, oils, and other greasy foods are hurtful. Cream is the most digestable form of fat, because it readily dissolves in the fluids of the stomach and mixes with the other foods without preventing their digestion. Melted fats are especially harmful. Cheese, fried foods, and rich pastry are very poor foods. Too much fat in the diet can lead to heart disease and other serious health problems.

7. Eating Too Many Kinds of Foods—Children should avoid eating flesh meats. They ought also to avoid eating all highly-seasoned dishes, and taking too many kinds of food at a meal. A simple diet is much the more healthful. Nut milks and grain foods, as oatmeal, cracked wheat, whole wheat bread, with such delicious fruits as apples, pears, and grapes, are some of the best foods.

8. Avoid Use of Cold Foods—We ought not to take very cold foods or liquids with our meals. Cold foods, ice water or iced tea, or to eat ice-cream at meals—these things are injurious to us at any time, but they do the greatest amount of harm when taken with the meal.

9. Things Sometimes Eaten Which Are Not Foods—Things which are not foods are often used as foods, such as mustard, pepper, and the various kinds of unhealthful seasonings. Baking soda, saleratus, and baking powders also belong to this class. All of these substances are more or less harmful, particularly mustard, pepper, and hot sauces.

10. Common Salt—The only apparent exception to the general rule that all condiments and other substances which are not foods are harmful is in the case of common salt. This is very commonly used among civilized nations, although there are many barbarous tribes that never taste it. It is quite certain that much more salt is used than is needed. When much salt is added to the food, the action of the digestive fluids is greatly hindered. Salt meats, and other foods which have much salt added to them, are hard to digest because the salt hardens the fibres of the meat, so that they are not easily dissolved by the digestive fluids.

11. Care of the Teeth—The teeth are used to chew the food, the first step in the work of digestion. It is of great importance that they should be kept in health. Many persons neglect their teeth and treat them so badly, that they begin to decay at a very early age.

12. The mouth and teeth should be carefully cleansed immediately on rising in the morning, and after each meal. All particles of food should be removed from between the teeth by carefully rubbing both the inner and the outer surfaces of the teeth with a tooth brush, and rinsing very thoroughly with water. A little tooth paste may be used in cleansing the teeth and should be used frequently and thoroughly. The teeth should not be used in breaking nuts or other hard substances. The teeth are brittle and are often broken in this way. The use of candy and too much sweet food is also likely to injure the teeth.

13. Some people think that it is not necessary to take care of the first set of teeth. This is a great mistake. If the first set are lost or are unhealthy, the second set will not be as perfect as they should be. It is plain that we should not neglect our teeth at any time of life.

14. Tobacco—When a person first uses tobacco, it is apt to make him very sick to his stomach. After he has used tobacco a few times it does not make him sick, but it continues to do his stomach and other organs harm, and after a time may injure him very seriously. Smokers sometimes suffer from a horrible disease of the lungs, mouth, or throat known as cancer.

15. Effects of Alcohol upon the Stomach—If you should put a little alcohol into your eye, the eye would become very red. When men take strong liquors into their stomachs, the delicate membrane lining the stomach becomes red in the same way. Perhaps you will ask, How do we know that alcohol has such an effect upon the stomach. More than sixty years ago there lived in Michigan a man named Alexis St. Martin. One day he was, by accident, shot in such a way that a large opening was made right through the skin and flesh and into the stomach. The good doctor who attended him took such excellent care of him that he got well. But when he recovered, the hole in his stomach remained, so that the doctor could look in and see just what was going on. St. Martin sometimes drank whiskey, and when he did, the doctor often looked into his stomach to see what the effect was, and he noticed that the inside of the stomach looked very red and inflamed.

16. If St. Martin continued to drink whiskey for several days, the lining of the stomach looked very red and raw like a sore eye. A sore stomach cannot digest food well, and so the whole body becomes sick and weak. What would you think of a man who should keep his eyes always sore and inflamed and finally destroy his eyesight by putting pepper or alcohol or some other irritating substance into them every day? Is it not equally foolish and wrong to injure the stomach and destroy one's digestion by the use of alcoholic drinks? Alcohol, even when it is not very strong, not only hurts the lining of the stomach, but injures the gastric juice, so that it cannot digest the food well.

17. Effects of Alcohol Upon the Liver—The liver, as well as the stomach, is greatly damaged by the use of alcohol. You will recollect that nearly all the food digested and absorbed is filtered through the liver before it goes to the heart to be distributed to the rest of the body. In trying to save the rest of the body from the bad effects of alcohol, the liver is badly burned by the fiery liquid, and sometimes becomes so shrivelled up that it can no longer produce bile and perform its other duties. Even beer, ale, and wine, which do not contain so much alcohol as do rum, gin, and whiskey, have enough of the poison in them to do the liver a great deal of harm, and to injure many other organs of the body as well.

SUMMARY

1. Causes of Indigestion:
Eating too fast;
Eating too much;
Eating too frequently;
Eating irregularly;
Eating when tired;
Eating too much of sweet foods;
Eating too many kinds of food at a meal;
Using iced foods or drinks.
2. Irritating substances and things which are not foods should not be eaten.
3. The teeth must be carefully used and kept clean.
4. Tobacco-using does the stomach harm, and sometimes causes cancer of the mouth.
5. Alcohol injures the gastric juice, and causes disease of the stomach and the liver.

Chapter 10

A Drop of Blood

1. The Blood—Did you ever cut or prick your finger so as to make it bleed? Probably you have more than once met with an accident of this sort. All parts of the body contain blood. If the skin is broken in any place the blood flows out.

2. How many of you know what a microscope is? It is an instrument which magnifies objects, or makes them look a great deal larger than they really are. Some microscopes are so powerful that they will make a little speck of dust look as large as a great rock.

3. The Blood Corpuscles—If you should look at a tiny drop of blood through such a microscope, you would find it to be full of very small, round objects called *blood corpuscles*.

4. You would notice also that these corpuscles are of two kinds. Most of them are slightly reddish, and give to the blood its red color. A very few are white.

5. Use of the Corpuscles—Do you wonder what these peculiar little corpuscles do in the body? They are very necessary. We could not live a moment without them. We need to take into our bodies oxygen from the air. It is the business of the red corpuscles to take up the oxygen in the lungs and carry it round through the body in a wonderful way, of which we shall learn more in a future lesson.

6. The white corpuscles have something to do with keeping the body well. They are carried by the blood into all parts of the body and stop where they find a foreign object. This may be a virus, bacteria, or it may be something like a sliver! The white corpuscles go to work fighting this foreign object to prevent infection and sickness.

7. The corpuscles float in a clear, almost colorless fluid, which contains the digested food and other elements by which the body is nourished.

SUMMARY

1. The blood contains very small objects called blood corpuscles.

2. There are two kinds of corpuscles, red and white.

3. The red corpuscles carry oxygen.

4. The white corpuscles repair parts that are worn.

5. The corpuscles float in a clear, almost colorless fluid, which nourishes the body.

Chapter 11

Why the Heart Beats

1. If you place your hand on the left side of your chest, you will feel something beating. If you cannot feel the beats easily, you may run up and down stairs two or three times, and then you can feel them very distinctly. How many of you know the name of this curious machine inside the chest, that beats so steadily? You say at once that it is the heart.

2. The Heart—The heart may be called a live pump, which keeps pumping away during our whole lives. If it should stop, even for a minute or two, we would die. If you will place your hand over your heart and count the beats for exactly one minute, you will find that it beats about seventy-five or eighty times. When you are older, your heart will beat a little more slowly. If you count the beats while you are lying down, you will find that the heart beats more slowly than when you are sitting or standing. When we run or jump, the heart beats much harder and faster.

3. Why the Heart Beats—We have learned in preceding lessons that the digested food is taken into the blood. We have also learned that both water and oxygen are taken into the blood. Thus the blood contains all the materials that are needed by the various parts of the body to make good the wastes that are constantly tak-

THE HEART

ing place. But if the blood were all in one place it could do little good, as the new materials are needed in every part of the body. There has been provided a wonderful system of tubes running through every part of the body. By means of these tubes the blood is carried into every part where it is required. These tubes are connected with the heart. When the heart beats, it forces the blood through the tubes just as water is forced through a pipe by a pump or by a fire-engine.

4. The Heart Chambers—The heart has four chambers, two upper and two lower chambers. The blood is received into the upper chambers, and is then passed down into the lower chambers. From the lower chambers it is sent out to various parts of the body.

5. The Blood Vessels—The tubes through which the blood is carried are called *blood vessels*. There are three kinds of blood vessels. One set carry the blood away from the hear, and are called **arteries** (ar'-te-ries). Another set return the blood to the heart and are called *veins*. The arteries and veins are connected at the ends farthest from the heart by many very small vessels. These minute, hair-like vessels are called *capillaries* (cap'-il-la-ries).

6. The Arteries—An artery leads out from the

lower chamber of each side of the heart. The one from the right side of the heart carries the blood only to the lungs. The one from the left side of the heart carries blood to every part of the body. It is the largest artery in the body, and is called the *aorta*. Soon after it leaves the heart the aorta begins to send out branches to various organs. These divide in the tissues again and again until they become so small that only one corpuscle can pass through at a time.

7. The Veins—These very small vessels now begin to unite and form larger ones, called veins. The small veins join to form larger ones, until finally all are gathered into two large veins which empty into the upper chamber of the right side of the heart. The veins which carry blood from the lungs to the heart empty into the upper chamber of the left side of the heart.

INSIDE THE HEART

8. What Is Done in the Blood Vessels—While the blood is passing through the small blood vessels in the various parts of the body, each part takes out just what it needs to build up its own tissues. At the same time, the tissues give in exchange their worn-out or waste matters. The red blood corpuscles in the capillaries give up their oxygen, and the blood receives in its stead a poisonous substance called carbon-dioxide.

9. Red and Blue Blood—While in the arteries the blood is of a bright red color; but while it is passing through the capillaries the color changes to a bluish red, or purple, color. The red blood is called *arterial blood*, because it is found in the arteries. The purple blood is called *venous blood*, because it is found in the veins. The loss of oxygen in the corpuscles causes the change of color.

10. Change of Blood in the Lungs—Exactly the opposite change occurs in the blood when it passes through the lungs. The blood which has been gathered up from the various parts of the body is dark, impure blood. In the lungs this dark blood is spread out in very minute capillaries and exposed to the air. While passing through the capillaries of the lungs, the blood gives up some of its impurities in exchange for oxygen from the air. The red corpuscles absorb the oxygen and the color of the blood changes from dark purple to bright red again. The purified blood is then carried back to the upper chamber of the left side of the heart through four large veins. The blood is now ready to begin another journey around the body.

11. The Pulse—If you place your finger on your wrist at just the right spot, you can feel a slight beating. This beating is called the *pulse*. It is caused by the movement of the blood in the artery of the wrist at each beat of the heart. The pulse can be felt at the neck and in other parts of the body where an artery comes near to the surface.

12. How Much Work the Heart Does—The heart is a small organ, only about as large as your fist, and yet it does an amount of work which is almost beyond belief. Each time it beats, it does as much work as your arm would do in lifting a large apple from the ground to your mouth. It beats when we are asleep as well as when we are awake. When we run we know by the way in which it beats that it is working very fast. Do you know how much a ton is? Well, in twenty-four hours the heart does as much work as a man would do in lifting stones enough to weigh more than one hundred and twenty tons.

13. The Lymphatics—While the blood is passing through the capillaries, some of the white corpuscles escape from the blood vessels. What do you suppose becomes of these runaway corpuscles? Nature has provided a way by which they can get back to the heart. In the little spaces among the tissues outside of the blood vessels very minute channels called *lymph channels* or *lymphatics* (lym-phat'-ics) begin. The whole body is filled with these small channels, which run together much like the meshes of a net. In the center of the body the small lymphatics run into large ones, which empty into the veins near the heart. This is the way the stray white blood corpuscles get back into the blood.

14. The Lymph—In the lymph channels the white corpuscles float in a colorless fluid called *lymph*. The lymph is composed of the fluid portion of the blood which has soaked through the walls of the small vessels. The chief purpose of the lymphatics is to carry the lymph from the tissues back to the heart.

15. Lymphatic Glands—Here and there, scattered through the body, are oval structures into each of which many lymphatic vessels are found to run, as shown in the illustration. These are called *lymphatic glands*.

16. The heart and blood vessels are among the most wonderful structures in the body. Proverbs tells us to "keep thy heart with all diligence; for out of it are the issues of life." While this is spiritually speaking, it is also true physically. It is no wonder, then, that alcohol, tobacco, and other narcotics and stimulants produce their most deadly effects upon these delicate organs. What these effects are we shall learn more fully in the next chapter.

LYMPH GLAND AND VESSELS

SUMMARY

1. The heart beats to circulate the blood.

2. The heart has four chambers, two upper and two lower.

3. There are tubes called blood vessels which carry the blood to all parts of the body.

4. These tubes are connected with the heart.

5. The vessels which carry blood away from the heart are called arteries, and those which carry blood back to the heart are called veins.

6. The arteries and veins are connected by small tubes called capillaries.

7. The blood found in the arteries is red; that in the veins is dark blue or purple.

8. The color of the blood changes from red to blue in going through the capillaries. The change is due to the loss of oxygen.

9. In the circulation of the lungs, the blood in the arteries is blue that in the veins, red.

10. The change from blue to red takes place while the blood is passing through the capillaries of the lungs. The change is due to the oxygen which the corpuscles of the blood take up in the lungs.

11. The pulse is caused by the beating of the heart.

12. The heart does a great deal of work every day in forcing the blood into different parts of the body.

13. Some of the white blood corpuscles escape from the blood vessels through the thin walls of the capillaries.

14. These corpuscles return to the heart through small vessels called lymph channels or lymphatics.

15. The lymphatics in many parts of the body run into small roundish bodies called lymphatic glands.

16. The object of the lymphatics is to remove from the tissues and return to the general circulation the lymph and white blood corpuscles which escape through the walls of the capillaries.

Chapter 12

A Healthy Heart and Pure Blood

1. The heart is one of the most important of all the organs of the body. If we take good care of it, it will do good service for us during a long life.

2. Violent Exercise—Did you ever run so hard that you were out of breath? Do you know why you had to breathe so fast? It was because the exertion of the muscles increased the amount of waste products which the blood carried to the lungs to exchange them for oxygen that was needed by the muscles to continue their work. When the exchange of gases in the lungs cannot keep up with the production of wastes in the muscles, you become winded, or out of breath.

3. Effects of Bad Air—Bad air is very harmful to the heart and to the blood also. We should always remember that the blood of the body, while passing through the lungs, is exposed to the air which we breathe. If the air is impure, the blood will be poisoned. In churches, classrooms, and in other places where many people are gathered, the air can become foul due to the large amounts of poisons exhaled and a lack of oxygen. In these situations, where people suffer from the want of God's fresh air, they become tired and sleepy. It is important that the air of the rooms in which we live and sleep should be kept very pure by good ventilation. Remember—the influence of pure, fresh air is to cause the blood to circulate healthfully through the body. The Old Testament has some interesting instruction given by God: "For the life of the flesh is in the blood." Leviticus 17:11.

Whatever pollutes the blood affects the life. This is true, not only of our physical life, but of our spiritual life also.

4. Effects of Bad Food—The blood is made from what we eat, and if we eat impure and unwholesome food, the blood becomes impure. We ought to avoid the use of rich or highly-seasoned foods, candies, and all foods which are not nutritious. They not only injure the blood by making it impure, but they cause poor digestion.

5. Plenty of Sleep Necessary—Our bodies need a proper amount of sleep, for it is during this time that the body more thoroughly cleanses itself of the wastes that have built up during a day of exercise.

6. Proper Clothing—We should be properly clothed, according to the weather. In cold weather we need very warm clothing. In warm weather we should wear lighter clothing. Our clothing should be so arranged that it will keep all parts of the body equally warm, and thus allow the blood to circulate properly. The feet are apt to be cold, being so far away from the heart, and we should take extra pains to keep them warm and dry.

7. Effects of Excessive Heat—In very hot weather many persons are injured by exposing themselves to the sun too long at a time. Persons who drink intoxicating liquors such as beer, wine, or other alcoholic beverages are very often injured in this way and become more susceptible to sunstroke.

8. Effects of Anger—When a person gets

very angry, the heart starts beating very fast and causes a strain on it. Indeed, persons have been known to have a heart attack due to a fit of passion. So you see it is not healthy for a person to allow himself to become very angry. We need to remember that Jesus will give us the strength to overcome anger.

9. Effects of Alcohol upon the Blood—If you should take a drop of blood upon your finger, put it under the microscope, and then add a little alcohol to it, you would see that the corpuscles would quickly be destroyed. In a few seconds they would be so shrivelled up that no one could tell that they had ever been the beautiful little corpuscles which are so necessary to health. When alcohol is taken as a drink, it does not destroy the corpuscles so quickly, but it injures them so that they are not able to do their work of absorbing and carrying oxygen well. A lack of oxygen can destroy the cells in our brains, therefore, if we wish to have a clear mind and a healthy body, we should never drink any form of alcohol.

10. Alcohol Overworks the Heart—Dr. Parkes, a very learned English physician, took the time to observe carefully the effects of alcohol upon the heart of a soldier who was addicted to the use of liquor. He counted the beats of the soldier's pulse when he was sober, and then counted them again then he was using alcohol, and found that when the soldier took a pint of gin a day his heart was obliged to do one fourth more work than it ought to do.

11. Effects of Alcohol upon the Blood Vessels—Alcohol causes the red blood cells to clump together. The small vessels which carry the blood from the arteries to the veins are only big enough for one red blood cell to pass at a time. When clumps of red blood cells start trying to go through these small vessels, called capillaries, they have to stretch to let the clumps through. It is this that causes the flushed cheeks and the red eyes of the drunkard. Sometimes, after a man has been using alcohol a long time, the blood vessels of his face remain enlarged

all the time. This often makes the alcoholic's nose swollen and red.

12. Effects of Tobacco on the Heart and the Blood—Oftentimes when a person first tries to use tobacco, it makes them feel very sick. If you should feel the pulse just then, you would find it very weak. This means that the heart is being affected by the powerful poison of the tobacco. Tobacco also injures the blood corpuscles.

13. *Tea* and *coffee* also do their share of mischief to the heart. Those who use them very strong often complain of palpitation, or heavy and irregular beating of the heart.

14. Taking Cold—People usually "catch a cold" by allowing the circulation to become disturbed in some way, as by getting the feet wet, being chilled from not wearing sufficient clothing, sitting in a draught, and in other similar ways. It is very important for you to know that a cold is a serious thing, and should be carefully avoided.

15. Hemorrhage (hem'-or-rhage) **or Loss of Blood**—A severe loss of blood is likely to occur as the result of accidents or injuries of various sorts, and it is important to know what to do at once, as there may not be time to send for a doctor before it will be too late to save the injured person's life. Here are a few things to be remembered in all such cases:

16. If the blood from a cut or other wound flows in spurts and is of a bright red color, it is from an artery. If it is dark-colored, and flows in a steady stream, it is from a vein.

17. How to Stop the Bleeding of Wounds—If the bleeding vessel is an artery, apply pressure on the side of the wound closest to the heart. If the bleeding is from a vein, apply it on the opposite side. It is generally best to apply pressure directly over the wound or on both sides. The pressure can be made with the thumbs or with the whole hand. Grasp the part firmly and press very hard, or tie a handkerchief or towel around the wounded part and twist it tight. If an arm or limb is the part injured, the person should be made to lie down, and the injured part should be held up. This is of itself an excellent means of stopping hemorrhage.

18. Nosebleed—Nosebleeds may be stopped by placing the hands and feet into water that is as hot as one can tolerate without causing burning. Another alternative to this is to place the hands and feet into ice water for four to six minutes. Either way, a cotton gauze should be placed in the nose with a small amount of petroleum jelly on it to soak up the blood. Pinching the nose for short periods of time with the head held forward is also effective.

SUMMARY

1. The blood carries waste gases from the muscles to the lungs, and oxygen from the lungs to the muscles.
2. Bad air makes the blood impure and is harmful to the whole body.
3. Unwholesome food produces bad blood.
4. Too little sleep makes the blood poor.
5. Proper clothing is necessary to make the blood circulate equally in different parts of the body.
6. Violent anger may cause stress on the heart.
7. Alcohol injures the blood.
8. Alcohol overworks the heart.
9. Alcohol enlarges the blood vessels.
10. Tobacco injures the blood.
11. Tobacco weakens the heart and makes the pulse irregular.
12. The use of strong tea and coffee causes palpitation of the heart.
13. A cold can be caused by a disturbance of the circulation. A cold should never be neglected.
14. When an artery is wounded, the blood is bright red and flows in spurts.
15. When a vein is wounded, the blood is purple and flows in a steady stream.
16. To stop bleeding from an artery, press on the side of the wound towards the heart, or on both sides of the wound.
17. When a vein is wounded, press on the side away from the heart.

Chapter 13

Why and How We Breathe

1. An Experiment—Let us perform a little experiment. We must have a small bit of candle, a fruit jar, or a bottle with a large mouth, and a piece of wire about a foot long. Notice carefully what we are about to do and what happens.

2. We will fasten the candle to the end of the wire. Now we will light it, and next we will let it down to the bottom of the jar. Now place the cover on the top of the jar and wait for the results. Soon the candle burns dimly, and in a little time the light goes out altogether.

3. What do you think is the reason that the candle will not burn when shut up in a bottle? A candle uses air when it burns. If shut up in a small, tight place, it soon uses up so much air that it can burn no longer. Try the experiment again, and when the candle begins to burn dimly, take it out quickly. We see that at once the light burns bright again.

4. Suppose we shut the wood stove's air control tight, what is the result? The fire will burn low, and after a time it will probably go out. Why is this? Evidently the stove needs air to make the wood or coal burn, just as the candle needs air to make it burn.

5. Animals Die Without Air—If you should shut up a mouse or any other small animal in a fruit jar, its life would go out just as the light of the candle went out. The little animal would die in a short time. A child shut up in a close place would die from the same cause in a very little time. In fact, many children die because they get locked in an old refrigerator or freezer, in which they use up all the available oxygen, causing suffocation.

6. Oxygen—The reason why animals need air, and why the fire will not burn without it, is that the air contains oxygen, and it is the oxygen in the air which causes the wood or coal to burn and produce heat. So it is the oxygen that burns in our bodies and keeps us warm.

7. When wood and coal are burned, heat is produced; but some parts of the fuel are not made into heat. While the fire burns, smoke escapes through the pipe or chimney; but a part of the fuel remains in the stove in the form of ashes. Smoke and ashes are the waste parts of the fuel.

8. Poison in the Breath—The burning which takes place in our bodies produces something similar to the smoke and ashes produced by the fire in a stove. The smoke is called *carbonic acid gas* [or, properly, *carbon dioxide*], an invisible vapor, and escapes through the lungs. The ashes are various waste and poisonous matters which are formed in all parts of the body. These waste matters are carried out of the body through the skin, the kidneys, the liver, and other organs.

9. Another Experiment—We cannot see the gas escape from our lungs, but we can make an experiment which will show us that it really does pass out. Get two drinking glasses and a tube. A glass tube is best, but a straw will do very well. Put a little clean water into one glass and the same quantity of limewater into the other glass. Now put one end of the tube into the mouth and place the other end in the pure water. Breathe through the tube a few times. Look at the water in the glass and see that no change has taken place. Now breathe through the limewater in the same way. After breathing two or three times, you will notice that the limewater begins to look milky. In a short time it becomes almost as white as milk. This is because the limewater catches the carbonic acid gas which escapes from our lungs with each breath, while the pure water does not.

10. Why We Breathe—By this experiment we learn another reason why we breathe. We must breathe to get rid of the carbon dioxide gas, which is brought to the lungs by the blood to be exchanged for oxygen. There are two reasons, then, why we breathe: (a) to obtain oxygen; (b) to get rid of carbon dioxide.

11. How a Frog Breathes—Did you ever see a frog breathe? If not, try to find the first opportunity to do so. You will see that the frog has a very interesting way of breathing. He comes to the top of the water, puts his nose out a little, and then drinks the air. You can watch his throat and see him swallowing the air, a mouthful at a time, just as you would drink water.

12. If you had a chance to see the inside of a frog you would find there an odd-shaped bag. This is his air bag. This bag has a tube running up to the throat. When the frog comes to the surface of the water he fills this bag with air. Then he can dive down into the mud out of sight until he has used up the supply of air. When the air has been changed to carbon dioxide gas, he must come to the surface to empty his air bag and drink it full again.

13. The Lungs—We do not drink air as the frog does, but like the frog we have an air bag in our bodies. Our air bag has to be emptied and filled so often that we cannot live underwater a long time, as a frog does. We call this air bag the lungs. We have learned before that the lungs are in the chest. We need so much air and have to change the air in our lungs so often that we would not have time to swallow it as a frog does. So nature has made for us a breathing apparatus of such a kind that we can

work it like a pair of bellows. Now, let's study our breathing-bellows and learn how they do their work.

14. The Windpipe and Air tubes—A large tube called the *trachea*, or more commonly called the *windpipe*, extends from the root of the tongue down the middle of the chest. The windpipe divides into two main branches, which subdivide again and again, until the finest branches are not larger than a sewing needle. The branches are called *bronchial tubes*. At the end of each tube is a cluster of small cavities called air cells. You will want to look at the picture, on the next page, that shows the air tubes and *air cells*. The air cells are broken down in many other parts that assist the blood in exchanging carbon dioxide with oxygen.

15. The Voice Box—If you will place the ends of your fingers upon your throat just above the breastbone, you will feel the windpipe, and may notice the ridges upon it. These are rings of cartilage, a hard substance commonly called *gristle*. The purpose of these rings is to keep the windpipe open. Close under the chin you can find something which feels like a lump, and which moves up and down when you swallow. This is a little box made of cartilage, commonly called the voice box, because by means of this curious little apparatus we are able to talk and sing. The technical name for this wonderful device given by our Creator is the *larynx*.

Two little white bands are stretched across the inside of the voice box. When we speak, these bands vibrate just as do the strings on a musical instrument. These bands are called the *vocal cords*.

16. The Epiglottis—At the top of the voice box is placed a curious trapdoor which can be shut down so as to close the entrance to the air passages of the lungs. This little door has a name rather hard to remember. It is called the *epiglottis* (ep-i-glot'-tis). The cover of the voice box closes whenever we swallow anything. This keeps food or liquids from entering the air passages. If we eat or drink too fast, the voice box will not have time to close its little door and prevent us from being choked. There have been cases of persons who have been choked to death by trying to swallow their food too fast. Isn't it amazing how our Creator made this very wonderful door that can open and shut just when it should do so without our thinking anything about it?

17. The Nostrils and the Soft Palate—The air finds its way to the lungs through the mouth or through the two openings in the nose called the *nostrils*. From each nostril three small passages lead backward through the nose. At the back part of the nasal cavity the passages of the two sides of the nose come together in an open space just behind the soft curtain which hangs down at the back part of the mouth. This curtain is called the *soft palate*. Through the opening behind this curtain the air passes down into the voice box and then into the lungs.

18. The Pleura—In the chest the air tubes and lung of each side are enclosed in a very thin covering called the *pleura*. The cavity of the chest in which the lungs are suspended is also lined by the pleura. A limpid fluid exudes from the pleura, which keeps it moist, so that when the two surfaces rub together as the lungs

——— VOICE-BOX

——— WINDPIPE

AIR-TUBES AND AIR-CELLS

move, they do not become chafed and irritated.

19. Walls of the Chest—The ribs form a part of the framework of the chest. The ribs are elastic. The spaces between them are filled up with muscles, some of which draw the ribs together, while others draw them apart. Can you tell any reason why the walls of the chest are elastic? The lower wall, or floor, of the chest cavity is formed by a muscle called the *diaphragm*, which divides the trunk into two cavities, the chest and the abdomen.

20. How We Use the Lungs—Now let's notice how we use the lungs and what actually takes place in them. Maybe you have seen an old fashion bellows. When using a pair of bellows, we take hold of the handles and draw them apart. The sides of the bellows are drawn apart so that there is more room between the sides. The air then rushes in to fill the space. When the bellows are full, we then press the handles together, and the air is forced out a small hole in the front.

21. It is in just this way that we breathe. When we are about to take a long breath, the muscles pull upon the sides of the chest in such a way as to draw them apart. At the same time the diaphragm draws itself downward. By these means, the cavity of the chest is made larger and air rushes in through the nose or mouth to fill the space. When the muscles stop pulling, the walls of the chest fall back again to their usual position, and the diaphragm rises. The cavity of the chest then becomes smaller, and the air is forced out through the nose or mouth. This process is repeated every time we breathe.

22. We breathe once for each four heartbeats. Small children breathe more rapidly than grown persons. We usually breathe about eighteen or twenty times in a minute.

23. How Much the Lungs Hold—Every time we breathe, we take into our lungs about two thirds of a pint of air and breathe out the same quantity. Our lungs hold, however, very much more than this amount. A man, after he has taken a full breath, can breathe out a gallon of air, or more than ten times the usual amount. After he has breathed out all he can, there is still almost half a gallon of air in his lungs which he cannot breathe out. So you see the lungs hold almost a gallon and a half of air.

24. Do you think you can tell why our Creator, Jesus Christ, has given us so much more room in the lungs than we ordinarily use in breathing? If you will run up and down stairs three or four times you will see why we need this extra lung-room. It is because when we exercise vigorously the heart works very much faster and beats harder, and we must breathe much faster and fuller to enable the lungs to purify the blood as fast as the heart pumps it into them.

25. The Two Breaths—We have learned that the air which we breathe out contains something which is not found in a very large quantity in the air which we breathe in. This is carbon dioxide gas. How many of you remember how we found this out? We can also tell this in another way. If we put a candle down in a wide jar it will burn for some time. If we breathe into the jar first, however, the candle will go out as soon as we put it into the jar. This shows that the air which we breathe out contains something which will put a candle out. This is carbon dioxide gas, which is heavier than oxygen and can suffocate a person if it becomes too concentrated.

26. The Breath—The air which we breathe out also contains many forms of impurities that the body is trying to throw off. These poisons make the air of a crowded or unventilated room smell very unpleasant to one who has just come in from the fresh air. Such air is not to breathe. Such a room also can contain many germs and other harmful bacteria.

27. The Lungs Purify the Blood—We have learned that the blood becomes dark in its journey through the body. This is because it loses its oxygen and receives carbon dioxide, which it has gathered up in the tissues, and takes up a new supply of oxygen, which restores its bright red color.

28. How the Air is Purified—Perhaps it occurs to you that with so many people and animals breathing, that after a time the air would become so filled with carbon dioxide that it would be unfit to breathe. This is prevented, once again, by a wonderful arrangement of our Creator. The carbon dioxide gas which can be poisonous to us is one of the most necessary foods for plants. Plants take in carbon dioxide through their leaves, and send the oxygen back into the air ready for us to use again.

29. We have already learned that the oxygen taken in by the lungs is carried to the various parts of the body by the little blood corpuscles. The effect of strong liquors will injure these corpuscles, so that they cannot carry so much oxygen as they ought to. For this reason the blood of a drunkard is darker in color than that of a temperate person, and contains more carbon dioxide. The drunkard's lungs may supply all the air he needs, but his blood has been so damaged that he cannot use it. Excessive smoking has a similar effect.

SUMMARY

1. Our bodies need air, just as a candle or a fire does.

2. A small animal shut up in a close jar soon dies for want of air. We need the oxygen which the air contains.

3. Oxygen causes a sort of burning in our bodies.

4. The burning in our bodies keeps us warm and destroys some of the waste matters.

5. The breathing organs are the windpipe and bronchial tubes, the voice box, the epiglottis, the nostrils, the soft palate, the lungs, the air cells, the pleura, the diaphragm, and the chest walls.

6. When we breathe, we use our lungs like a pair of bellows.

7. A man's lungs hold nearly one and a half gallons of air.

8. In ordinary breathing we use less than a pint of air, but when necessary we can use much more.

9. The air we breathe out contains carbon dioxide gas and other invisible poisons.

10. A candle will not burn in air which has been filled with our breath, and animals die when confined in such air.

11. The lungs purify the blood. While passing through the lungs, the color of the blood changes from purple to bright red.

12. Plants purify the air by removing the carbon dioxide.

13. Alcohol and tobacco injure the blood corpuscles, so that they cannot take up the oxygen from the air which the lungs receive.

Chapter 14

How to Keep the Lungs Healthy

1. Pure Air Necessary—A person may go without eating for a month, or without drinking for several days, and still live; but a strong man will die in minutes if deprived of air. It is very important that we breathe plenty of pure, fresh air. There are many ways in which the air becomes impure.

2. Bad Odors and Chemicals—Anything which rots or decays will in so doing produce an unpleasant odor. Bad odors produced in this way are very harmful and are likely to make us sick. Many people have rotting potatoes and other vegetables in their cellars, and heaps of refuse in their backyards. These are all dangerous to health, and often give rise to very serious disease. We should always remember that bad odors caused by decaying substances are signs of danger to health and life, and that these substances should be removed from us, or we should stay away from them as much as possible. That is why it is wise to place a compost pile a good distance from our homes.

Also, many of the things we use, such as spray paint, glue, and other chemicals, can be very harmful to the lungs and should be avoided as much as possible.

3. Germs—The chief reason why bad odors are dangerous is that they almost always have with them little living things called *germs*. Germs are so small that they cannot be seen by the naked eye; it takes a strong microscope to enable us to see them; but they are so powerful to do harm that if we receive them into our bodies they are likely to make us very sick, and can even cause death.

4. Contagious Diseases—You have heard about diphtheria and scarlet fever and measles and other "catching diseases." When a person is sick with one of these diseases, the air about him is poisoned with germs, or something similar, which may give the same disease to other persons who inhale it. Therefore, when a person is sick from one of these diseases, it is very important that he should be put in a room by himself and be shut away from everyone but the doctor and the nurse. It is also necessary that all the clothing and bedding used by the sick person, and everything in the room, as well as the room itself, be carefully cleansed and disinfected when the person has recovered, so as to wipe out every trace of the disease. The writer has known many cases in which persons who have been sick with some of these diseases were careless and gave the disease to others who died of it, although they themselves recovered. Do you not think it very wrong for a person to give to another through carelessness a disease which may cause his death?

5. Unhealthful vapors and odors of various sorts can arise from damp, closed-up places under a house. Rooms which are shaded and shut up so tight that fresh air and sunshine seldom get into them should be well aired and warmed before used to live in.

6. Ventilation—The only way to obtain the amount of fresh air needed, when we are shut up indoors, is to have some means provided by which the fresh air shall be brought in and the old and impure air carried out. Changing the air by such means is called *ventila-*

tion. Every house, and especially every sleeping room, should be well ventilated. Schoolhouses, churches, and other places where many people gather, need good ventilation. Ask your teacher to show you how the schoolroom is ventilated; and when you go home, talk to your parents about the ventilation of the house in which you live.

7. Many people ventilate their houses by opening the doors and windows. This is a very good way of ventilating a house in warm weather; but is a very poor way in cold weather, as it causes cold drafts and makes the floor cold, so that it is difficult to keep the feet warm. It is much better to have the air warmed by a furnace, or some similar means, before it enters the rooms. There ought also to be in each room a register to take the foul air out, so that it will not be necessary to open the window. This register should be placed at the floor, because when the pure air enters the room warm, it first rises to the upper part of the room, and then as it cools and at the same time becomes impure, it settles to the floor, where it should be taken out by the register.

8. **How to Breathe**—We should try to make an effort to expand the lungs well in breathing, and to use the entire chest, both the upper and the lower part. Clothing should be worn in such a way that every portion of the chest can be expanded. For this reason it is not wise to wear the clothing extremely tight about the waist. Clothing so worn is likely to hinder the lungs from operating properly.

9. **Bad Habits**—We should always use great care to sit erect and to draw the shoulders well back. Then, if we remember to try to fill the lungs full many times every day, we shall form the habit of expanding the lungs, and shall breathe deeper, even when we are not thinking about doing so.

10. **Breathing Through the Nose**—In breathing, we should always take care to draw the air in through the nose, and not through the mouth. The nose acts as an air cleaner, to remove particles of dust which might do harm if allowed to enter the lungs. It also warms and moistens the air in cold weather. The habit of breathing through the mouth often gives rise to serious disease of the throat and lungs.

11. **Effects of Alcohol and Tobacco Upon the Lungs**—Both alcohol and tobacco produce disease of the breathing organs. Smoking injures the throat and sometimes causes loss of smell. Smoking can also cause lung and throat cancer and emphysema. Alcohol is damaging to every organ of the body; for it contaminates the blood, consequently, it, too, is very harmful to the lungs.

12. Many people suppose that the use of alcohol will save a man from getting sick. This is not true. A man may become a drunkard by the use of alcohol, and yet he is more likely to get sick than he would have been if he had been a total abstainer. "Alcoholism" is one of the most dreadful forms of disease a person can suffer.

SUMMARY

1. Pure air is as necessary as food and drink.

2. Anything which is rotting or undergoing decay causes a bad odor, and thus makes the air impure.

3. Foul air contains germs which cause disease and sickness.

4. Persons sick with "catching" diseases should be carefully avoided. Such persons should be shut away from those who are well, and their rooms and clothing should be carefully cleansed and disinfected.

5. We should change the air in our houses, or ventilate them, so that we may always have pure air.

6. We should always keep the body erect, and expand the lungs well in breathing.

7. The clothing about the chest and waist should be loose, so that the lungs may have room to expand.

8. Always try to breathe through the nose.

9. Tobacco causes disease of the throat, nose, and lungs.

10. Alcohol is damaging to all the organs of the body, including the lungs.

Chapter 15

The Skin and What it Does

1. The Skin—The skin is the covering of the body. If you use your fingers to pinch a little fold of the skin, you will see that it can be stretched like a piece of rubber. Like rubber, when it is released it quickly snaps back and appears as before.

2. The Bark of Trees—Did you ever peel the bark off of a young tree? If so, you have noticed that there were really two barks, an outer bark, as thin as paper, through which you could almost see, and an inner and much thicker bark, which is next to the wood of the tree. You can peel off this very thin outer bark without doing the tree much harm. Indeed, if you will notice some of the fruit or shade trees in the yard at home, you will see that the outer bark of the tree peels itself off a little at a time, and that new bark grows in its place. If you tear off the inner bark, which goes down to the wood, it will injure the tree. It will make it bleed, causing the sap to run out of the injury. The sap is the blood of the tree. The bark is the skin of the tree. When the bare place heals over, an ugly scar will be left.

3. The Cuticle—Our bodies, like trees, have two skins or really one skin with an outer and an inner layer. When a person burns himself so as to make a blister, the outer skin, called the *cuticle*, is separated from the inner by a quantity of water, or serum, poured out from the blood. This causes the blister to rise above the surrounding skin. If you puncture the blister the water runs out. Now we may easily remove the cuticle and examine it. The cuticle, we shall find, looks very much like the skin which lines the inside of an egg-shell, and it is almost as thin.

4. The cuticle is very thin in most parts of the body, but in some places, as the palms of the hands and the soles of the feet, it is quite thick. This is because these parts of the skin come in contact with objects in such a way as to be liable to injury if not thus protected. The cuticle has no blood vessels and very few nerves. With a fine needle and thread you can easily take a stitch in it without making it bleed or causing any pain.

5. The Pigment—The underside of the cuticle is colored by little particles of pigment, or coloring matter. The color of this pigment differs in different races. In the Negro, the color of the pigment is black. In some races the pigment is brown. In white persons there is very little pigment, and in some persons, called albinos, there is none at all.

6. The Inner or True Skin—The inner skin, like the inner bark of a tree, is much thicker than the outer skin. It is much more important, and for this reason is sometimes called the *true skin*. It contains nerves and blood vessels.

7. The Sweat Glands—If you look at the palm of the hand you will see many coarse lines, and by looking much closer you will see that the palm is completely covered with very fine ridges and furrows. Now, if you examine these ridges with a magnifying glass, you will find arranged along each ridge a number of little dark spots. Each of these points is the

SKIN OF PALM OF HAND MAGNIFIED

mouth of a very small tube. This is called a *sweat duct*. These ducts run down through both the outer and inner layers of the skin. At the underside of the true skin the end of the tube is rolled up in a coil, as you can see by looking at the illustration. The coiled parts of the tubes are called *sweat glands*, because they separate from the blood the fluid that we call sweat, or perspiration.

8. The Oil Glands—There are other little glands in the skin which make fat or oil. The oil is poured out upon the skin to keep it soft and smooth.

9. The Hair—There are some curious little pockets in the skin. Out of each of these pockets grows a hair. On some parts of the body the hairs are coarse and long; on other parts they are fine and short.

10. Many of the ducts leading from the oil glands open into the pockets or pouches from which the hairs grow. The oil makes the hair soft and glossy. Nature has thus provided an excellent means for oiling the hair.

11. The hair is chiefly useful as a protection. It is also an ornament.

12. The Nails—The nails of the fingers and the toes grow out of little pockets in the skin just as the hairs do. Both the hair and the nails are really parts of the outer skin, which is curiously changed and hardened. The nails lie upon the surface of the true skin and grow from the underside, as well as from the little fold of skin at the root of the nail. They are made to give firmness and protection to the ends of the fingers and toes. The nails of the fingers are also useful in picking up small

objects and in many other ways.

13. Uses of the Skin—The skin is useful in several ways:

(1) *It Removes Waste*—The sweat glands and ducts are constantly at work removing from the blood particles which have been worn out and can be of no further use. If we get very warm, or if we run or work very hard, the skin becomes wet with sweat. In a little while, if we stop to rest, the sweat is all gone. What becomes of it? It has evaporated, which means that it has passed off into the air. Sweating is going on all the time, but we do not sweat so much when we are quiet and are not too warm, and so the sweat evaporates as fast as it is produced, and we do not see it. This is one of the marvelous ways that God designed to keep our body

THE STRUCTURE OF THE SKIN

temperature cooler while doing hard work on a hot day. Nearly a quart of sweat escapes from the skin daily.

(2) *Breathing Through the Skin*—We breathe to a slight extent through the skin. There are some lower animals which breathe with their skins altogether. A frog, for instance, breathes through its skin. A frog can breathe with its skin so well, that it can live for some time after its lungs have been removed. Breathing is an important part of the work of the skin, and we should be careful, by keeping it clean and healthy, to give it a good chance to breathe all that it can.

(3) *The Skin Absorbs*—The skin absorbs many substances which come in contact with it, and hence should be kept clean. If the foul substances which are removed in the sweat are allowed to remain upon the skin, they may be taken back into the system and thus do much harm.

(4) *The Skin Has Feeling*—When anything touches the skin, we know it by the feeling. We can tell a great many things about objects by feeling of them. If we happen to stick a pin into the skin, we feel pain. We are also able to tell the difference between things which are hot and those which are cold. Thus the sense of feeling which the skin has is very useful to us.

(5) *The Skin Protects the Body*—The skin is a natural clothing which protects us much better than any other kind of clothing could. It is so soft and pliable that it cannot hurt the most delicate part which it covers, yet it is very strong and tough.

SUMMARY

1. The skin is the covering of the body. It has two layers, the outer, called the cuticle, and the inner, called the true skin.

2. A substance called pigment is found between the two skins. This gives the skin its color.

3. The true skin has blood vessels and nerves, but the cuticle has not blood vessels and very few nerves.

4. In the true skin are glands which produce sweat, and others which make fat, or oil.

5. The nails are really a part of the skin. They are firm and hard, and protect the ends of the fingers and the toes.

6. The hair grows from the true skin. The hair is made soft and glossy by oil from the oil glands of the skin.

7. The skin is a very useful organ. It removes waste matters, it breathes, it absorbs, it has feeling, and it protects the body.

Chapter 16

How to Take Care of the Skin

1. Uses of the Pores of the Skin—Many years ago, at a great celebration, a little boy was covered all over with varnish and gold leaf, so as to make him represent an angel. The little boy looked very pretty for a short time, but soon he became very sick, and in a few hours he was dead. There were two reasons: The pores absorbed the chemicals from the varnish. and the pores of his skin were stopped up, so that they could not carry off the poisonous matter from his body.

2. Cleanliness—Did you ever know of a boy who had his skin varnished? Probably not, but there are people in some countries who do not wash their skin as often as they should, and the sweat, oil, and dead skin form a sort of varnish which stops up the little ducts and prevents the air from getting to the skin, almost as much as a coat of varnish would do.

3. The Sweat Glands—The sweat glands and ducts are like little sewer pipes made to carry away some of the impurities of the body. There are so many of them that, if they were all put together, they would make a tube two or three miles long. These little sewers drain off almost a quart of impurities in the form of sweat every day. So you see that it is very important for the skin to be kept clean and healthy.

4. Bathing—A bird takes a bath every day. Dogs and many other animals like to go into the water to bathe. Some of you have seen a great elephant take a bath by showering the water over himself with his trunk. To keep the skin healthy we should bathe frequently.

5. When we take a bath for cleanliness it is good idea to use a little soap, so as to remove the oil which is mixed up with the dry sweat, dead skin, and dirt which may have become attached to the skin.

6. It is not good to take extremely hot baths all the time, but they are very helpful in treating certain sicknesses. A frequent warm bath or shower is the best way to keep the skin clean and healthy.

7. The Clothing—The skin should be protected by proper clothing, but it is not well to wear more than is necessary, as it makes the skin so sensitive that one is liable to take cold.

8. The Proper Temperature of Rooms—It is also very unwise for a person to keep the rooms in which he lives too warm, and to stay too much indoors, as it makes him very liable to take cold when he goes out of doors. One who is out of doors in all kinds of weather seldom takes cold.

9. Care of the Hair and the Nails—The scalp should be kept clean by thorough and frequent washing with shampoo and daily brushing.

10. The habit of biting and picking the fingernails is a very disagreeable one, and keeps the nails broken and unhealthy. The nails should be carefully trimmed with a pair of nail clippers.

11. Effects of Narcotics and Stimulants

Upon the Skin—Alcohol, tobacco, opium, and all other narcotics and stimulants have a bad effect upon the skin. Alcohol often causes the skin to become red and blotched, and tobacco gives it a dingy and unhealthy appearance.

SUMMARY

1. If the pores of the skin are closed, the body will not be able to throw off poisons as well.

2. We should bathe often enough to keep the skin clean.

3. We should not keep our rooms too warm, and should avoid wearing too much clothing. We should also keep our limbs evenly clothed, especially in cold weather.

4. Alcohol, tobacco, and other stimulants and narcotics injure the skin.

Chapter 17

The Kidneys and Their Work

1. The Kidneys_The kidneys are among the most important organs of the body, They are in the cavity of the abdomen, near the backbone, up under the lower border of the ribs.

2. The Work of the Kidneys—The work of the kidneys is to separate from the blood certain very poisonous substances, which would soon cause our death if they were not removed. It is very important to keep these useful organs in good health, because a person is certain to die very soon when the kidneys are in any way seriously injured.

3. How to Keep the Kidneys Healthy—One way of keeping the kidneys in good health is to drink plenty of pure water, and to avoid eating meat and rich food. Pepper, mustard, vinegar, and other hot sauces are very harmful to kidneys.

KIDNEY

4. Importance of Keeping the Skin Clean—The work of the kidneys is very similar to that of the skin; and when the skin does not do its full duty, the kidneys have to do more than they should, and hence are likely to become diseased. For this reason, persons who allow their skins to become inactive by neglecting to bathe frequently are apt to have disease of the kidneys.

5. Effects of Alcohol and Tobacco Upon the Kidneys—A piece of beef placed in alcohol soon becomes dry and hard, and shrivels up as though it has been burned. The effect upon the kidneys of one who drinks strong liquor is almost the same. Beer and wine also do the kidneys harm, sometimes producing incurable disease of these important organs.

SUMMARY

1. The kidneys somewhat resemble the skin in their work.

2. The kidneys remove from the blood some poisonous substances.

3. To keep the kidneys healthy we should drink plenty of water, avoid irritating foods and drinks, and keep the skin in health by proper bathing.

4. The drinking of strong liquors often causes incurable disease of kidneys.

Chapter 18

Our Bones and their Uses

1. The Bones—In an earlier chapter we learned something about the bones. This we must try to recall. You will remember that we called the bones the framework of the body, just as the timbers which are first put up in building a house are called its frame.

2. The Skeleton—All the bones together make up the *skeleton*. There are about two hundred bones in all. They are of many different shapes. They vary in size from the little bones of the ear, which are the smallest, to the upper bone of the leg, which is the largest in the body.

3. The skeleton is divided into four parts: the *skull*, the *trunk*, the *arms*, and the *legs*. We must learn something more about the bones of each part.

4. The Skull—The *skull* is somewhat like a shell. It is made of a number of bones joined together in such a way as to leave a hollow place inside to hold the brain. The front part of the skull forms the framework of the face and the jaws. In each ear there are three curious little bones, which aid us in hearing.

5. The Trunk—The bones of the trunk are, the *ribs*, the *breastbone*, the *pelvis*, and the *backbone*. The bones of the trunk form a framework to support and protect the various organs within its cavities.

6. The Ribs—There are twelve *ribs* on each side. The ribs join the backbone at the back. They are connected by cartilage to the breastbone in front. With the breastbone and the backbone they form a bony cage to contain and protect the heart and the lungs.

7. The Pelvis—The pelvis is at the lower part of the trunk. It is formed by three bones closely joined together. The large bones at either side are called the hipbones. Each hipbone contains a deep round cavity in which the upper end of the thighbone rests.

8. The Backbone—The *backbone*, or *spinal column*, is made up of twenty-four small bones, joined together in such a way that the whole can be bent in various directions. The skull rests upon the upper end of the spinal column. The lower end of the backbone forms a part of the pelvis.

9. The Spinal Canal—Each of the separate bones that make up the backbone has an opening through it, and the bones are so arranged, one above another, that the openings make a sort of canal in the backbone. By the connection of the spinal column to the head this canal opens into the cavity of the skull. Through this canal there passes a peculiar structure called the *spinal cord*, of which we shall learn more at another time.

10. The Arms—Each of the arms has five bones, besides the small bones of the hand. They are the *collarbone*, which connects the shoulder to the breastbone, the *shoulder blade*, at the back of the shoulders, the *upper arm bone*, between the shoulder and the elbow, and the two *lower arm bones*, between the elbow and the wrist. There are eight little bones in the wrist, five in that part of the hand next to the wrist, and fourteen in the fingers and thumb.

11. The Legs—The bones of the leg are the

thigh or *upper leg bone*; the *kneepan* or *kneecap*, which covers the front of the knee; the two bones of the *lower leg*; the *heel bone* and six other bones in the *ankle*; five bones in that part of the foot next to the ankle; and fourteen bones in the *toes*.

12. Use of the Bones—The skeleton is not only necessary as a framework for the body, but it is useful in other ways. Some of the bones, as the skull, protect delicate parts. The brain is so soft and delicate that it would be very unsafe without its solid bony covering. The spinal cord also needs the protection which it finds in the strong but flexible backbone. The bones help to move our hands and arms, and assist us in walking.

13. The Joints—The places where two or more bones are fastened together are called **joints**. Some joints we can move very freely, as those of the shoulder and the hip. Others have no motion at all, as those of the bones of the skull.

14. Cartilage—The ends of bones which come together to form a joint are covered with a smooth, tough substance, which protects the bone from wear. This is called *gristle* or *cartilage*. You may have seen the gristle on the end of a soupbone or on one of the bones of a joint of beef.

15. The joint contains a fluid to oil it, so that

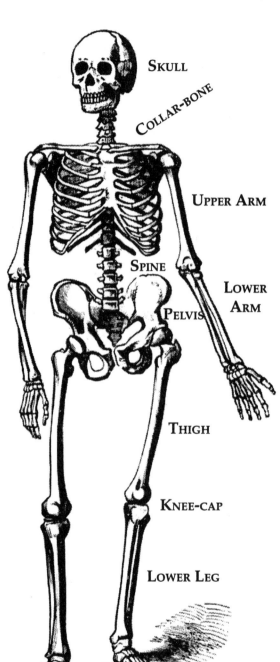

SKULL
COLLAR-BONE
UPPER ARM
SPINE
LOWER ARM
PELVIS
THIGH
KNEE-CAP
LOWER LEG

SKELETON OF A MAN

the ends of the bones move upon each other very easily. If the joints were dry, every movement of the body would be very difficult and painful.

16. The bones are held together at the joints by means of strong bands called *ligaments*.

17. How the Bones are Made—The bones are not so solid as they seem to be. The outside of most bones is much harder and firmer than the inside. Long bones, like those of the arms and the legs, are hollow. The hollow space is filled with *marrow*, in which are the blood vessels which nourish the bone.

18. An Experiment—If you will weigh a piece of bone, then burn it in the fire for several hours, and then weigh it again, you will find that it has lost about one third of its weight. You will also notice that it has become brittle, and that it seems like chalk.

19. Why the Bones Are Brittle—The hard, brittle portion of a bone which is left after it has been burned contains a good deal of calcium and other minerals. It is this which makes the bones so hard and firm that they do not bend by the weight of the body. When we are young, the bones have less of these minerals, which makes the bones softer, and so they bend easily and readily get out of shape. When we get old, the bones again start losing these minerals, causing them to become more brittle, and often they break very easily. One of the benefits of a vegetarian diet is that in old age the bones lose their calcium much more slowly.

SUMMARY

1. There are about two hundred bones in the body.
2. All together they are called the skeleton.
3. The skeleton is divided as follows:
    a. The Skull
    b. The Trunk
Ribs   Breastbone   Pelvis   Backbone
    c. The Arms
Collarbone   Shoulder blade
Upper arm bones
Lower arm bones
Wrist   Hand and fingers
    d. The Legs
Thigh   Kneepan
Lower leg bones
Ankle, including heel bone
Foot and Toes
4. The bones are useful for support, protection, and motion.
5. The place where the bones join is called a joint.
6. The tough substance which covers the ends of many bones is called cartilage or gristle.
7. The joints are enabled to work easily by the aid of a fluid secreted for that purpose.
8. The ends of the bones are held together in a joint by means of ligaments.

48

Chapter 19

How to Keep the Bones Healthy

1. Composition of the Bones—Our bones, like the rest of our bodies, are made of what we eat. If our food does not contain enough of the substances needed to make healthy bone, the bones will become unhealthy. They may be too soft and become bent or otherwise misshapen. This is one of the reasons why bread made from the whole grain is so much more healthful than that made from very fine white flour. In making fine white flour the miller takes out the very best part of the grain, just what is needed to make strong and healthy bones. Oatmeal is a very good food for making healthy bones, as well as dark green vegetables.

2. Improper Position—We should not allow ourselves to take improper positions in sitting, lying, or standing. This is the way uneven shoulders, curved spines, and many other deformities can be caused over many years. Always try to stand up straight, and do not slouch when you sit down.

3. Broken Bones—By rough play or by accident the bones may be broken in two, just as you might break a stick. If the broken parts are placed right, our Creator will cement them together and make the bone strong again; but sometimes the bones do not unite, and sometimes they grow together out of proper shape, so that permanent injury is done.

4. Sprains—In a similar manner the ligaments which hold the bones together in a joint are sometimes torn or overstretched. Such an accident is called a sprain. A sprain is a very painful accident, and a joint injured in this way needs to rest quite a long time, so that the torn ligaments may grow together.

5. Bones out of Joint—Sometimes the ligaments are torn so badly that the ends of the bones are displaced, and then we say they are put out of joint. This is a very bad accident indeed, but it often happens to boys while wrestling or playing at other rough games.

6. Children sometimes pull the fingers to cause the knuckles to "crack." This is a very foolish and harmful practice. It weakens the joints and causes them to grow large and unsightly.

7. When a man uses alcohol and tobacco, their effects upon the bones are not so apparent as are the effects upon the blood, the nerves, and other organs; but when the poisonous drugs are used by a growing boy, their damaging influence is very plainly seen. A boy who smokes cigars or cigarettes, or who uses strong alcoholic liquors, is likely to be so stunted that even his bones will not grow to a proper length and he will become dwarfed.

SUMMARY

1. For the bones to stay healthy they must have plenty of healthful food.

2. The whole-grain preparations and dark green vegetables furnish the best food for the bones.

3. The bones may be easily broken or put out of joint, or the ligaments may be torn by rough play.

4. Alcohol prevents healthy growth.

Chapter 20

The Muscles and How We Use Them

1. The Muscles—Many people in the world eat meat. Where does this meat come from? From the grocery store, you may say. But where does the store get it? From the various animals which are killed and used for that purpose. But what does most of this meat consist of? The muscles of an animal. If you will squeeze your arm you will notice that the bones are covered by a soft substance, which is your meat, or muscle. When the skin of an animal has been taken off, we can see that some of the flesh is white or yellow and some of it is red. The white or yellow part is usually fat. The red part is meat, and it is composed of muscles.

2. The Number of Muscles—We have about five hundred different muscles in the body. They are arranged in such a way as to cover the bones and make the body round and beautiful. They are of different forms and sizes.

3. With a very few exceptions the muscles are arranged in pairs; that is, we have two alike of each form and size, one for each side of the body.

4. How a Muscle is Formed—If you could examine a piece of meat carefully, you would notice that it seems to be made up of bundles of small fibers or threads of flesh. With a little care you could pick one of the small fibers into fine threads. Now, if you look at one of these under a microscope, you find that it is

MUSCULAR FIBRES

made of still finer fibers, which are much smaller than the threads of a spider's web. One of these smallest threads in called a *muscular fiber*. Many thousands of muscular fibers are required to make a muscle.

5. Most of the muscles are attached to the bones. Generally, one end is attached to one bone, and the other to another bone. Sometimes one end is connected to a bone and the other to the skin or to other muscles.

6. The Tendons—Many of the muscles are not joined to the bones directly, but are attached to them by means of firm cords called *tendons*. If you will place the thumb of your left hand upon the wrist of the right hand, and then work the fingers of the right hand, you may feel these cords moving underneath the skin.

7. What the Muscles Do—With the left hand grasp the right arm just in front of the elbow. Now shut the right hand tightly. Now open it. Repeat several times. The left hand feels something moving in the flesh. The motion is caused by the working of the muscles, which shorten and harden when they act.

8. All the movements of the body are made by means of muscles. When we move our hands, even when we close the mouth or the eyes, or make a smiling face, we use the muscles. We could not speak, laugh, sing, or breathe without muscles.

9. Self-acting Muscles—Did you ever have a fit of sneezing or hiccoughing? If you ever did, very likely you tried hard to stop but could not. Do you know why one cannot always stop sneezing or hiccoughing when he desires to do so? It is because there are certain muscles in the body which do not act simply when we wish them to act, but when it is necessary that they should. The muscles which act when we sneeze or hiccough are of this kind. The arm and the hand do not act unless we wish them to do so. Suppose it were the same with the heart. We should have to stay awake all the while to keep it going, because it would not act when we were asleep. The same is true of our breathing. We breathe when we are asleep as well as when we are awake, because the breathing muscles work even when we do not think about them.

10. The stomach, the intestines, the blood vessels, and many other organs within the body have this kind of muscles. The work of these self-acting muscles is very wonderful indeed. Without it we could not live a moment. This knowledge should lead us to consider how dependent we are, each moment of our lives, upon the delicate machinery by which the most important work of our bodies is performed, and how particular we should be to keep it in good order by taking proper care of ourselves. Every breath we take, every beat of our heart, is God's wonderful gift of life to each of us. Isn't the body He has given us a wonderful thing!

SUMMARY

1. Meat is usually composed of muscles.

2. There are five hundred muscles in the body.

3. Muscles are composed of many small threads called muscular fibers.

4. Many of the muscles are joined to the bones by strong white cords called tendons.

5. Muscular fibers can contract so as to lessen their length. It is in this way that the muscles perform their work.

6. All bodily motions are due to the action of the muscles.

7. Most of the muscles act only when we wish them to do so. Some muscles, however, act when it is necessary for them to do so, whether we will that they should act or not. Thus they can function when we are asleep, as well as when we are awake.

Chapter 21

How to Keep the Muscles Healthy

1. How to Make the Muscles Strong—If you are right-handed, with which hand can you lift the more? with the right hand or with the left? Why do you think you can lift more with the right hand than with the left? A carpenter swings a heavy hammer with his right arm, and that arm becomes slightly larger and stronger than his left. If we wish our muscles to grow large and strong, so that our bodies will be healthy and vigorous, we must get plenty of exercise.

2. Effects of Idleness—If a person should carry one hand in his pocket all the time and use only the other hand and arm, the idle arm would become small and weak, while the other would grow large and strong. Any part of the body that is not used will after a time become weak. Boys and girls who do not get enough exercise are likely to be pale and small. It is important that we should take the proper amount of exercise every day, just as we take our food and drink every day.

3. Healthful Exercise—Some kinds of play, and almost all kinds of work which children have to do, are good ways of taking exercise. A very good kind of exercise for little boys and girls is that found in running errands or doing chores about the house. Then when these are done, there is always plenty of running, swinging, and ball catching that can be done out of doors.

4. Food and Strength—A great part of our food goes

FOOT OF CHINESE WOMAN

to nourish the muscles. Some foods make us strong, while others do not. Plain foods, such as bread, vegetables, potatoes, and nuts, are good for the muscles; but rich cakes, candy, pop, and other things which are not food, such as mustard, pepper, and harmful spices, do not give us strength, and are not the best for the bodies that God has given us.

5. Overexertion—We ought not to exert ourselves too much in lifting heavy weights, or trying to do things which are way too hard for us. Sometimes the muscles are permanently injured in this way.

6. The Clothing—We ought not to wear our clothing so tight as to press hard upon any part of the body. If we do, it will cause the muscles in that part of the body not to work as well. If the clothing is worn too tight about the waist, harm can be done. The lungs cannot expand properly, the stomach and liver are pressed out of shape, and the internal organs are crowded out of their proper places.

7. Tight Shoes—People are often made very lame from wearing tight shoes. Their muscles cannot act properly, and their feet grow out of shape.

8. Years ago in China it was fashionable for rich ladies to have small feet. They would tie them up in cloths so that they could not grow. The foot was squeezed out of shape. Here is a picture of a foot which has been treated in this way. It does not look much like a human foot, does it? A woman who has such feet finds it so difficult to walk that she has to be carried about much of the time. Do you not think it is very wrong and foolish to treat the feet so badly? You will say, "Yes;" but the Chinese woman thinks it is a great deal worse to lace the clothing very tight about the body so as to make the waist small.

9. Effects of Alcohol Upon the Muscles— When an intemperate man takes a glass of strong drink, it makes him feel strong; but when he tries to lift, or to do any kind of hard work, he cannot lift so much nor work so hard as he could have done without the liquor. This is because alcohol poisons the muscles and makes them weaker.

10. Effects of Drunkenness—When a man has become addicted to strong drink, his muscles become partly paralyzed, so that he cannot walk as steadily or speak as readily or as clearly as before. His fingers are clumsy, and his movements uncertain. If he is an artist or a jeweller, he cannot do as fine work as when he is sober. When a man gets very drunk, sometimes he will "pass out," and he is then for a time completely paralyzed, so that he cannot walk or move, and seems almost like a dead man.

11. If you had a good horse that had carried you a long way in a carriage, and you wanted to travel farther, what would you do if the horse were so tired that he kept stopping in the road? Would you let him rest and give him some water to drink and some nice hay and oats to eat, or would you strike him hard with a whip to make him go faster? If you should whip him, he would act as though he were not tired at all, but do you think the whip would make him strong, as rest and hay and oats would?

12. When a tired man takes alcohol, it acts like a whip; it makes every part of the body work faster and harder than it ought to work and thus wastes the man's strength and

makes him weaker, although for a little while his nerves are numb, so that he does not know that he is tired and ought to rest.

13. When you grow up to be men and women, you will want to have strong muscles. So you must be careful not to give alcohol a chance to injure them. If you never taste it in any form you will be sure to suffer no harm from it. Remember—"Know ye not that your body is the temple of the Holy Ghost which is in you, which ye have of God, and ye are not your own?" 1 Corinthians 6:19. God has given us a wonderful house to live in.

14. Effects of Tobacco on the Muscles— Young boys who smoke cigars or cigarettes, or who chew tobacco, are not likely to grow up to be strong and healthy men. They often do not have the tone and vigor of other boys or young men.

15. The evil effect of tobacco upon young people is now so well known that laws have been made which do not allow alcohol or tobacco to be sold or given to people under a certain age. This should make a person aware of the harmful effects of these poisons on the body. When we use alcohol, tobacco, or any other hurtful drug, we rob our constitution of its vigor, and steal away from us the strength that we need as we grow older.

16. Tea and Coffee—Tea containing caffeine, and coffee, while by no means so bad as alcohol and tobacco, may still cause us health problems. A person who drinks strong tea or coffee feels less tired while at work than if he had not taken it, but he is more tired afterwards. So you see that tea and coffee are also whips, small whips we might call them, and yet they really act in the same way as do other narcotics and stimulants. They make a person feel stronger than he really is, and thus he is led to use more strength than he can afford to do.

SUMMARY

1. We must use the muscles to make them grow large and strong.

2. Exercise should be taken regularly.

3. Exercise makes the muscles strong, the body beautiful, the lungs active, the heart vigorous, and the whole body healthy.

4. Things we ought not to do: run or play hard just before or after eating; strain our muscles by lifting too heavy weights; lie, sit, stand, or walk in a cramped position, or awkward manner; wear the clothing so tight as to press hard upon the muscles.

5. Good food is necessary to make the muscles strong and healthy.

6. Alcohol makes the muscles weak, although at first it makes us feel stronger.

7. A boy who uses tobacco will not grow as strong and well as one who does not.

8. The use of strong tea and coffee may injure the muscles.

Chapter 22

How We Feel and Think

1. How We Think—With what part of the body do we think? You will at once say that we think with our head; but we do not think with the whole head. Some parts of the head we use for other purposes, as the mouth to eat and speak with, and the nose to smell and breathe with. The part we think with is inside of the skull, safely placed in a little room at the top part of the head. Do you remember the name of this organ which fills the hollow place inside of the skull? We learned some time ago that it is called the *brain*. It is with the brain that we study and remember and reason. So the brain is one of the most important organs in our body, and we must try to learn all we can about it.

2. The Brain—You cannot see and examine your own brain, because it is in your skull; but you can get some idea what it looks like by examining the picture on this page.

3. The Higher Brain and the Lower Brain—In examining a brain we should notice first of all that there are really two brains, a large *upper brain* called the *cerebrum* and a smaller *lower brain* consisting of the *cerebellum*, the *thalamus*, and the *hypothalamus*. The upper brain is in the top of the skull, and the lower one lies beneath the back part of the larger one. If we look again

THE BRAIN

we shall see that each brain is divided in the middle into a right and a left half. Each half is, in fact, a complete brain, so that we really have two pairs of brains.

4. Brain Cells—The brain is a curious organ of a grayish color outside and white inside. It is soft, almost like jelly, and this is why it is placed so carefully in our skull, which is like a strong, bony box. If we should put a little piece of the brain under a microscope, we should find that it is made up of a great number of very small objects called *nerve* or *brain cells*. In the illustration you can see some of these brain cells.

5. The Nerves—Each cell has one or more branches. Some of the branches are joined to the branches of other cells so as to unite the cells together, just as children take hold of one another's hands. Other branches are drawn out very long.

6. The long branches are such slender threads that a great number of them together would not be as large as a fine silk thread. A great many of these fine nerve threads are bound up in little bundles which look like white cords. These are called *nerves*. These nerves are like little electrical wires that run throughout the whole body.

7. The nerves branch out from the brain

BRAIN CELLS

through openings in the skull, and go to every part of the body. Every little muscle fiber, the heart, the stomach, the lungs, the liver, even the bones—all have nerves coming to them from the brain. So you see that the brain is not wholly locked up in the skull, because the nerves connected to it have slender branches running into all parts of the body; and thus the brain itself is really in every part of the body, though we usually speak of it as being entirely in the skull. It is by this means that the brain can communicate to the rest of the body.

8. The Spinal Cord—There are a number of small holes in the skull through which the nerves pass out, but most of the nerves are bound up in one large bundle and pass out through an opening at the back part of the skull and run downward through a long canal in the backbone. This bundle of nerves forms the *spinal cord*. The spinal cord also contains cells like those of the brain. It is really a continuation of the lower brain down through the backbone.

9. Nerves from the Spinal Cord—Nerves branch out from the spinal cord, going to the arms, the chest, the legs, and other parts. One of the branches which goes to the hand runs along the back side of the arm, passing over the elbow. If we happen to strike the elbow against some sharp object, we sometimes hit this nerve. When we do so, the underside of the arm and the little finger feel very numb and strange. This is why you call this part of the elbow the "crazy bone," or the "funny bone." The cells of the spinal cord also send out

branches to the body and to other cells in the brain.

10. How We Feel—If we cut or burn ourselves we suffer pain. Can you tell why it hurts to prick your skin with a pin, or to pinch or burn or bruise it? It is because the skin contains a great many nerve branches from the brain. When we hurt the skin or the flesh in any way, these nerves are injured. There are so many of these little nerves in the flesh and skin that we cannot put the finest needle into the flesh without hurting some of them.

11. The Use of Pain—It is not pleasant for us to have pain, but if we did not feel pain when we are hurt we might get our limbs burned or frozen and know nothing about it until too late to save them. Our wonderful Creator has built an alarm system into our body for this very reason.

12. Nerves of Feeling—We have different kinds of nerves of feeling. Those we have learned about feel pain. Others feel objects. If you take a marble or a pencil in the hand, you know what it is by the feeling of the object. This kind of feeling is called the sense of touch.

13. There are other nerves of feeling, by means of which we are able to hear,

LARGE BRAIN

SMALL BRAIN

SPINAL CORD

BRAIN AND SPINAL CORD

see, taste, and smell, of which we shall learn in another lesson. Besides these we have nerves which tell us whether objects are cold or hot, and heavy or light. Nerves of feeling also tell us when we are hungry, or thirsty, or tired, and when we need more air to breathe.

14. Nerves of Work—There are other nerves which are made just like the nerves of feeling, but which do not feel. These nerves have a very different use. They come from cells in the brain which have charge of the different kinds of work done in the body, and they send their branches to the parts which do the work; hence we call them *nerves of work.*

15. One set of cells sends nerves to the heart, and these make it go fast or slow as is necessary. Another sends nerves to the liver, stomach, and other digestive organs, and causes them to do their part in the digestion of the food. Other cells send branches to the muscles and make them act when we wish them to do so. Thus you see how very useful the brain and nerves are. They keep all the different parts of the body working together in harmony, just like a well-trained army, or a great number of workmen building a block of houses. Without the brain and nerves the body would be just like an army without a commander, or a lot of workmen without a foreman.

16. How We Use the Nerves—If you happen to touch your hand to a hot stove, what takes place? You will say that your arm pulls the hand away. Do you know why? Let us see. The nerves of feeling in the hand tell the nerve cells in the spinal cord from which they come that the hand is being burned. The cells which feel cannot do anything for the hand, but in the spinal cord their message is relayed to the brain and to the nerves connected to the muscles of the arm. The nerves in this reflex circuit send the message down their various branches and cause the muscles to contract. The cells of feeling ask the cells which have charge of the muscles to make the muscles of the arm pull the hand away,

which they do very quickly, and the response is much quicker, because the message doesn't need to travel all the way to the brain first.

17. So you see the nerves are very much like telephone wires. By means of them the brain finds out all about what is happening in the body, and sends out its orders to the various organs, which may be called its servants.

18. An Experiment—A man once tried an experiment which seemed very cruel. He took a dove and cut open its skull and took out its upper portion of the brain. What do you think the effect was? The dove did not die at once, as you would expect. It lived for some time, but it did not know anything. It did not know when it was hungry, and would not eat or drink unless the food or water was placed in its mouth. If a man gets severely struck on his head so hard as to break his skull causing the upper brain to be damaged so badly that its cells cannot work, the man can end up in the same condition as the poor dove. He does not know anything. He cannot think or talk, and lies as though he were asleep.

19. By these and many other facts we know that the upper brain is the part with which we remember, think, and reason. It is also through the brain that the Holy Spirit speaks to us. It is the seat of the mind. We go to sleep because the large brain is tired and cannot work any longer. We stop thinking when we are sound asleep, but sometimes we do not sleep soundly, and then the large brain works a little and we dream.

20. What the Lower Brain Does—The lower brain, which we have already mentioned, consists of such structures as the cerebellum, the thalamus, and the hypothalamus. It thinks too, but it does not do the same kind of thinking as the large upper brain. We may use our arms and legs and many other parts when we wish to do so; and if we do not care to use them we may allow them to remain quiet. This is not the case with some other organs. It is necessary, for example, that the heart, the lungs, and many other organs of the body should keep at work all the time. If the upper brain had to attend to all of these different kinds of work besides thinking about what we see, hear, and read, and other things which we do, it would have too much work to do, and would not be able to do it all well. Besides, the upper brain sometimes falls asleep. So God has designed that the lower brain should do the kinds of work which have to be attended to all the time, so the lower brain keeps steadily at work when we are asleep as well as when we are awake. The lower brain also regulates hunger, thirst, sleep and other basic behaviors.

21. What the Spinal Cord Does—If you tickle a person's foot when he is asleep, he will pull it up just as he would if he were awake, only not quite so quickly. What do you suppose makes the muscles of the leg contract when the brain is asleep and does not know that the foot is being tickled? And here is another interesting fact. When you were walking about this morning, you did not have to think about every step you took. Perhaps you were talking or looking at different things; but your legs walked right along all the time, and without your thinking about them. How could this be?

22. It would be too much trouble for the upper brain to stop to think every time we step, so the lower brain co-operates in keeping the feet walking. Reflex action, such as pulling up the feet if someone should tickle them while we are asleep, is taken care of in a circuit to and from the spinal cord. The sensory nerves in the feet feel the tickling and send a message to the spinal cord. In turn the spinal cord relays the message to the nerves which tell the muscles to move the feet away from that which is tickling them.

SUMMARY

1. The part of the body with which we think is the brain.
2. The brain is found filling the hollow place in the skull.
3. There are two brains, the upper brain and the lower brain.
4. Each brain is divided into two equal and complete halves.
5. The brain is largely made up of very small nerves.
6. The nerve cells send out very fine branches which form the nerves.
7. The nerve branches or fibers run to every part of the body.
8. Most of the nerve branches pass out through a large opening at the back of the skull, in one large bundle called the spinal cord.
9. The spinal cord runs down through a canal in the backbone, and all along gives off branches to the various parts of the body.
10. It gives us pain to prick or hurt the flesh in any way, because when we do so we injure some of the little nerves which are connected to the brain.
11. When we hurt, it is really in the brain that we become aware we feel pain.
12. We have different kinds of nerves of feeling.
13. There are nerves of work.
14. The nerves of work have charge of the heart, the lungs, the muscles, the liver, the stomach, and every part of the body which can work or act.
15. The brain and nerves control the body and make all the different parts work together in harmony.
16. The brain uses the nerves very much as a man uses the telephone wires.
17. With the upper brain we remember, think, and reason.
18. The lower brain does the simple kind of thinking, by means of which the heart, lungs, and other vital organs are kept at work even when we are asleep.
19. The spinal cord does a still more simple kind of work. It serves as the relay center between the senses of feeling and the nerves controlling the muscles. The name we give these automatic responses is reflexes.

Chapter 23

How to Keep the Nerves Healthy

1. Uses of the Brain—What do you think a boy or girl would be good for without any brain or nerves? Such a boy or girl could not see, hear, feel, talk, run about, or play, and would not know any more than a cabbage or a potato knows. The mind is one of the most amazing gifts that God has given us. It is "with the mind" that we "serve the law of God." Romans 7:25. Your mind makes you everything you are—your thoughts, feelings, and decisions. It is through our mind that God speaks to us. In all that we do, we need the Holy Spirit dwelling in us. If we welcome Him into our heart, or, in other words, our mind, we will be obeying the instruction of Paul: "Be not conformed to this world: but be ye transformed by the renewing of your mind." Romans 12:2. The transforming power of Christ changes our characters—our thoughts, decisions, and feelings. Our part is to will and to choose; His part is to do through us.

2. The Brain Sympathizes With Other Organs—Have you ever had a headache? Did you feel happy and cheerful when your head ached real bad? Could you study and play as well as when you were feeling good? It is very important that we should keep our brain and nerves healthy, and to do this we must take good care of the stomach and all other organs, because the brain sympathizes with them when they are sick. Remember, God communicates to us through our minds. We can, then, understand how important it is to keep the body healthy, so that our minds will be also healthy and clear.

3. We Must Have Pure Air—How do you feel when the schoolroom is too warm and close? Do you not feel dull and sleepy, so that it becomes hard to study? This is because the brain needs good, pure blood to enable it to work well. So we must always be careful to have plenty of pure air to breathe.

4. We Should Exercise the Brain—What do we do when we want to strengthen our muscles? We make them work hard every day, do we not? The exercise makes them grow large and strong. In just the same way, if we study hard and learn our lessons well, then our brains grow strong, and study becomes easier. But if we become lazy, and do not take the time to learn our lessons well, then the study does not do our brains very much good.

5. We Should Take Muscular Exercise—When you get tired of study, an hour of play or exercise of some sort rests you and makes you feel more alert, so that you can learn more easily. This is because exercise is necessary to make the blood circulate well. It will then supply the brain and nerves with fresh, pure blood. So the same exercise that makes our muscles strong makes our brains healthier also.

6. We Should Be Careful of Our Diet—We ought to eat plenty of good, simple food, such as fruits, nuts, grains, and vegetables. It is not well for children to eat the flesh of dead animals, as it places a burden on the whole system to digest it. It simply is not the best for health. Mustard, pepper, and all hot sauces and other harmful spices have a tendency to irritate the brain and nerves.

7. We Should Allow the Brain to Rest at the Proper Time—When we are tired and sleepy, we cannot think well and cannot remember what we learn if we try to study. If we have plenty of sleep we awake in the morning rested and refreshed, because while we have been asleep our Creator has put the brain and nerves in good repair for us. We ought not to stay up too late at night. It is said that one hour of sleep before midnight is worth two hours after midnight. We should not eat late evening meals or snacks, as this will prevent our sleeping well.

8. We Ought Not to Allow Ourselves to Become Angry—When a person flies into a passion, it is not healthy for the brain and nerves. God can give us strength to overcome bad tempers, and we will be much happier and healthier.

9. We Should Shun Bad Habits—Bad habits are very hard to give up, and hence we should be careful to avoid them. As we just said, God is always there to help us in overcoming them. It is our choice, and if we do choose God's will and way, He will supply the strength. When a young person learns to swear, or to use slang phrases, the brain after a while will make him swear or use bad words before he thinks. In a similar manner other bad habits are acquired. It is much better never to learn these habits from the start.

SUMMARY

1. A person without a brain or nerves would be of no more account than a vegetable.

2. When the brain or nerves are sick they cannot perform their duties properly.

3. To keep the brain and nerves in good health, we must take good care of the stomach and all other important organs of the body.

4. There are many things which we may do to keep the brain and nerves strong and well.

5. The brain needs pure blood, and so we must be careful to breathe pure air.

6. The brain gets strength by exercise, just as the muscles do. Hence, study is healthful and makes the brain strong.

7. A good memory is very necessary, so we should learn to memorize.

8. It is very important that we learn how to observe things closely.

9. Exercise in the open air rests and clears the brain by helping the blood to circulate.

10. Plenty of wholesome and simple food is necessary to keep the brain and nerves in good health. Harmful spices, condiments, and rich foods in general are stimulating and are not healthy.

11. Plenty of sleep is needed to rest the brain and nerves.

12. It is not good to become real angry.

13. We should be careful to avoid forming bad habits of any sort, as they are hard to break, and often adhere to one through life.

Chapter 24

Effect of Alcohol on Brain and Nerve

1. Drunkenness—Did you ever see a man who was drunk? If you live in a city it is very likely that you have. How did the drunken man behave? Perhaps he was noisy and silly. Perhaps he was angry and tried to pick a fight with someone.

2. What made the man drunk? You say whiskey, wine, or beer that he drank. Anything that contains alcohol will make a man drunk, for it is the alcohol which causes the problem.

3. The Whiskey Flush—You can almost always tell when a man has been drinking, even when he has not taken enough to make him drunk. You know by his flushed face and red eyes. When a man's face blushes from the use of alcohol, his whole body blushes at the same time. His muscles, his lungs, and his liver blush; his brain and spinal cord blush also.

4. When a man has taken just enough alcohol to make his face blush a little, the extra amount of blood in the brain makes him think and talk more lively, and he can be very cheerful and happy. This makes many people think that alcohol does them good. But if we notice what a man says when he is under the influence of alcohol, we shall find that his remarks are often very silly and careless. He says very unwise and foolish things, for which he feels sorry when he becomes sober.

5. Alcohol Paralyzes—How does a drunken man walk? Let us see why he staggers. When a man takes a large amount of alcohol his brain and spinal cord become partly paralyzed, so that they cannot do their work properly, and

so, when he tries to walk he reels and stumbles along, often falling down, and sometimes even hurting himself. The fact is that the alcohol has put his spinal cord and brain in kind of a sleep so that he cannot make his legs do what he wants them to do. Now, if still more alcohol is taken the brain can become so effected that the man will become so drunk that he will "pass out" and look as if he is dead, that is why some say he is "dead drunk." It is very harmful to organs of your body to become dead drunk. Especially does it affect the brain, destroying thousands of important brain cells that help us to think, as well as function.

6. A small amount of alcohol does not make a man dead drunk, but it still poisons and paralyzes his brain and nerves just according to the quantity he takes.

7. If a person holds a little alcohol in his mouth for a few moments, the tongue and cheeks feel numb. This is because the alcohol paralyzed them so that they cannot feel or taste. When taken into the stomach, it has much the same kind of effect upon the nerves of the whole body.

8. Alcohol a Deceiver—A hungry man takes a drink of whiskey and benumbs the nerves of his stomach so that he does not feel hungry. Alcohol puts to sleep the sentinels which Christ our Creator has placed in the body to warn us of danger. A man who is cold takes alcohol and feels warm, though he is really colder. He lies down in his false comfort and can freeze to death. A tired man takes his glass of strong drink, beer, or wine, and feels rested and strong, though he is really weaker than before. A poor man gets drunk and feels so rich that he spends what little money he has. The alcohol paralyzed his judgment and steals away his good sense. Thus alcohol is always a deceiver.

9. Delirium Tremens (De-lir'-i-um Tre'-mens.)—When a man takes strong liquors regularly, he very soon injures his brain and nerves, so that they are very irritated, and at night he can not sleep well. He has frightful dreams. He sees all sorts of wild animals and horrid shapes in his dreams. Perhaps you have sometimes had such dreams from eating big late suppers or hard-to-digest food.

10. Did you ever have a dream when you were awake? If a man drinks a great deal he is likely to have a terrible disease known as *delirium tremens*, in which he sees the same frightful things when he is wide awake that he dreams about when he is asleep. This is one of the terrible effects of alcohol upon the brain and nerves.

11. Alcohol Paralysis—You have seen how a drunken man staggers when he walks. Did you ever see a man who walked just as though he were drunk when he was really sober? This is because a part of the brain or spinal cord has been permanently injured or paralyzed. Alcohol is not the only cause of this disease, and so you must not think every person who staggers is or has been a drunkard; but alcohol can cause this problem.

12. Effects of Alcohol Upon the Mind and Character—When a man is under the influence of alcohol, is his character good or bad? Is a man likely to be good, or to be bad, when he is drunk or excited by drink? Most men behave badly when they are drunk, and after they have been drunk a great many times they often behave badly all the time. A great many of the men who are shut up in prisons would not have been sent there if they had never learned to drink. Since Christ would have us to form good characters, it would be wise for us to avoid anything that will hurt us and cause us to do bad things.

13. A Legacy—Do you know what a legacy is? If your father should die and leave to you a fine house or farm, or money in the bank, or books, or automobiles, or any other kind of property to have for your own, it would be a legacy. When a person gets anything in this way from a parent we say that he inherits it.

14. We inherit a great many things besides houses and lands and other kinds of property. For instance, perhaps you remember hearing someone say that you have eyes and hair the same color as your mother's, and that your nose and chin are like your father's. So you have inherited the color of your hair and eyes from your mother and the shape of your chin and nose from your father.

15. The Alcohol Legacy—The inside of a boy's head is just as much like his parents' as the outside of it. In other words, we inherit our brains just as we do our faces. So, if a man spoils his brain with alcohol and gets an alcohol appetite, his children will be likely to have an appetite for alcohol also, and may become drunkards. Is not that a dreadful kind of legacy to inherit?

16. Wise physicians will tell you that one reason why tobacco is bad for you is that it can cause lung cancer. It also hurts your brain so that you cannot work as well, and because of this it hinders you from being able to do as well in life as you would have, had never used such poisons.

17. Tobacco Leads to Vice—Young people who use tobacco are more liable to get into company with other young people who have other bad habits, and so are apt to become bad in many other ways. The use of tobacco often makes people want to drink, and thus leads to drunkenness. It may also lead you into company with those who use drugs. All these things are out to hurt you. If you wish to grow up with a healthy body, a strong heart, and a good character you will leave tobacco and other such drugs alone.

18. Effects of Tea and Coffee on the Nerves—People who use strong tea and coffee are often inclined to be nervous. This shows that strong tea and coffee, like alcohol and tobacco, are very injurious to the nerves.

19. Prescription Drugs—There are several drugs which are given by physicians to relieve pain or to produce sleep. They are sometimes helpful, but abuse of these is very dangerous. The danger is that, after a person has used the medicine a little while, he will continue to use it. If a person takes a poisonous drug every time he has a little pain, he will soon form the habit of using it, and may never break it off. There are many thousands of people who use drugs all the time, and they are very much injured by it in mind and body. The mind becomes dull and the body weak and feeble. No medicine of this sort should ever be taken, unless prescribed by a physician.

SUMMARY

1. In order to be well and useful, we must keep the brain and nerves healthy.

2. To keep the brain healthy, we need plenty of pure air to breathe; proper exercise of the brain by study; sufficient exercise of the muscles in play and work; plenty of good food to make pure blood; a proper amount of rest and sleep.

3. We should not read or study too much. We should not allow ourselves to become overly excited or angry. We should avoid learning bad habits.

4. Alcohol paralyzes the brain and nerves.

5. Alcohol deceives a person who takes it by making him feel strong when he is weak; warm when he is cold; rich when he is poor; well when he is sick.

6. Alcohol demoralizes. Many men who commit crimes are men who use liquor.

7. The effects of tobacco upon the brain and nerves are much the same as those of alcohol. Tobacco is injurious to the mind.

8. Tobacco using often leads young people to drunkenness and other drugs.

Chapter 25

Hearing, Sight, Smell, Taste, and Touch

1. The Senses—God has given us have five senses—*hearing, seeing, smelling, tasting,* and *feeling*. These are called special senses because they are very different from each other. They also differ from the general sense of feeling by means of which we feel pain when any part is hurt.

2. Organs of the Special Senses—Each of the special senses has a special set of nerves and also special cells in the brain which have charge of them. We say that we see with our eyes, hear with our ears, feel with our fingers, et cetera; but, really, we see, hear, taste, and smell in the brain, just as we feel in the brain. The eyes, ears, nose, and other organs of the special senses are the instruments by means of which the brain sees, hears, smells, et cetera.

3. Sound and the Vibrations Which it Causes—All sounds are made by jars or vibrations of objects. Sounds cause objects to vibrate or tremble. A loud sound sometimes jars a whole house, while other sounds are so gentle and soft that we cannot feel them in the same way that we feel loud sounds. But our Creator has made for us an ingenious organ, by means of which we can feel these very fine vibrations, as well as loud ones. We call this organ the ear.

THE EAR

4. The Ear—The part of the ear which we can see is shaped somewhat like a trumpet and is called the *outer ear*. The small opening near the middle of the ear leads into a *canal*, or tube, which extends into the head about an inch. At the inner end there is a interesting little chamber. This is called the *middle ear*. At the end of the canal of the ear there is stretched a thin membrane like the head on a drum, and, in fact, it is called the *eardrum*. The middle ear is located behind this drum.

5. Bones of the Ear—Within the middle ear there are three very interesting little bones, which are joined together so as to make a complete chain, reaching from the eardrum to the other side of the middle ear. The last bone fits into a little hole which leads into another interesting chamber. This chamber, which is called the *inner ear*, is filled with a fluid. It is here that sound comes to the nerves and is then transmitted to the brain. A part of the inner ear looks very much like a snail shell.

6. How We Hear—Take a long wooden pole or good sized stick, and scratch it with a spoon or some other hard object. While you are doing this, have someone listen with the ear placed close against the other end of the stick. Ask him what he hears. He will tell you that he hears the scratching sound very plainly. This is because the scratching sound goes through the pole to the ear. The sound travels down the ear canal and vibrates the eardrum. When the eardrum vibrates it moves the bones of the ear, and these carry the vibration to the nerves in the inner ear. The nerves com-

EAR BONES OF
MIDDLE EAR

INNER EAR

EXTERNAL EAR

THE INSIDE OF THE EAR

municate the sound to the brain, where we understand it to be a scratching sound. Amazing, isn't it! We hear all sounds in the same way, only most sounds come to the ear through the air instead of through a stick.

7. How to Keep the Ears Healthy—The ears are very delicate organs and must be carefully treated. The following things about the care of the ears should never be forgotten:

(1.) Never use a pin, toothpick, or any other sharp instrument to clean out the ear. There is great danger that the eardrum will be punctured, and thus the hearing will be injured.

(2.) Do not allow cold wind to blow directly into the ear.

(3.) If anything accidentally gets into the ear, do not work at it, but hold the head over to one side while water is made to run in from a syringe. If an insect has gone into the ear, pour in a little olive or mineral oil. This will kill the insect or make it come out.

(4.) Never shout into another person's ear. The ear may be greatly injured in this way. In fact, try your best to avoid any loud sound. If you must work around noisy equipment, it is a good idea to wear ear plugs to keep your ears from being damaged. Loud music can also damage your ears.

Hearing is one of the most precious gifts that God has given us, and we should do all that we can to protect it.

8. The Eye—The eye is one of the most wonderful organs in the whole body. It enables us to know what is going on around us and to enjoy many beautiful things which our sense of hearing and other senses can tell us nothing about. It also enables us to read. Let us learn about this wonderful organ that our Creator has given us.

9. The Eyeball—Looking at the eye, we see first a round part which rolls in different directions. This is the eyeball. We see only the front side of the eyeball as it fits into a hollow in the skull. Being thus in a safe place, it is not likely to get hurt.

The eyeball is mostly filled with a clear substance very much like jelly. It is so clear that the light can shine through it just as easily as it can shine through water.

10. The Pupil—If you look closely at the eyeball you will see a small black hole just in the center. This is a little window which lets the light into the inside of the eyeball. We call this the *pupil*. Just around the pupil is a colored ring which gives the eye its color. We say a person has blue or brown or gray eyes according as this ring is blue or brown or gray. This colored ring is a kind of curtain for the window of the eye.

11. If you observe the pupil closely, you will see that it is sometimes larger and sometimes smaller. If you look at the light, the pupil is small; if you turn away from the light, the pupil grows larger at once. This is because the curtain closes when in a bright light and opens in the darkness. It does this of itself without our thinking about it. In this way the eye is protected from too strong a light, preventing great harm.

12. If you look a little sideways at the eyeball, you will see that the curtain has something in front of it which is clear as glass. In fact, this is the window to the eye. We will talk more about this window in just awhile.

13. The White of the Eye—The white of the eye is a tough, firm membrane which encloses the eyeball and keeps it in a round shape.

14. Do you know what a lens is? Perhaps you do not know it by this name, but you are familiar with the glasses which people wear to help their eyes to see better. The glasses are made up of frames and lenses; the lens being the part you look through. Well, there is something in the eye almost exactly like one of these lenses, only smaller. It is also called a *lens*. If you could take apart a camera, you would find that it has a lens too, and works much like the eye. The lens is placed in the eyeball just behind the pupil. (See picture.)

THE EYE

15. The Nerves of Sight—But a person might have an eyeball with all the parts we have learned about and yet not be able to see. Can you tell what more is needed? There must be a nerve. This nerve comes from some little nerve cells in the brain and enters the eyeball

at the back of the eye; there it is spread out on the inside of the black lining of the white of the eye. This membrane which contains the nerves is called the *retina* (ret'-i-nah).

16. The Eyelids—Now we know all that it is necessary for us to learn about the eyeball, so let us notice some other parts about the eye. First there are the eyelids. They are little folds of skin, which we can shut up so as to cover the eyeball and keep out the light when we want to sleep or when we are in danger of getting dust or smoke into the eye. The eyelids are fringed with hairs placed along the edge of the lids to help keep the dust out when the eyes are open. The eyelids also help to keep the eye moist. This is why we blink from time to time.

17. The Eyebrows—The row of hairs placed above the eye is called the eyebrow. Like the eyelids, the eyebrows catch some substances which might fall into the eye, and they also serve to turn off the perspiration and keep it out of the eyes.

18. The Tear Gland—Do you know where the tears come from? There is a little gland snugly placed away in the socket of the eye just above the eyeball, which makes tears in the same way that the salivary glands make saliva. It is called the *tear gland*. The gland usually makes just enough tears to keep the eye moist. There are times when it makes more than enough, as when something gets into the eye, or when we suffer pain or feel unhappy. Then the tears are carried off by means of a little tube which runs down into the nose from the inner corner of the eye. When the tears are formed so fast that they cannot all get away through this tube, they pass over the edge of the lower eyelid and flow down the cheek.

19. Muscles of the Eyes—By means of little muscles that are fastened to the eyeball, we are able to turn the eye in almost every direction.

20. How We See—Now we want to know how we see with the eye. This is not very easy to understand, but we can learn something about it. Let's do an experiment. Take a glass lens, such as a magnifying glass, hold it before a window and place a piece of smooth white paper behind it on the side away from the window. If you move the glass back and forth till an image is focused on the paper, you will be able to see a picture on the paper of whatever

THE INSIDE OF THE EYE

is outside the window. The picture made by the lens looks exactly like the view out-of-doors, except that it is upside down. This is one of the interesting things that a lens does. The lens of the eye acts just like the glass lens. It makes a picture upon the retina of everything we see. The nerves in the retina transfer the picture spread out at the back of the eyeball to the brain. This is how we see.

21. Did you ever look through a set of binoculars or a telescope? If so, you know you must focus on the object you are looking at by making the telescope a little longer or shorter. The eye also has to be changed a little when we look from near to distant objects. Look out of the window at a tree a long way off. Now place a lead pencil between the eyes and the tree. You can scarcely see the pencil while you look closely at the tree, and if you look at the pencil you cannot see the tree distinctly.

22. There is a little muscle in the eye which makes the change needed to enable us to see objects close by as well as those which are far-

ther away. When people grow old the little muscles cannot do this so well, and hence old people sometimes have to put on glasses to see objects near by, as in reading.

23. How to Keep the Eyes Healthy— One of the ways to keep the eyes healthy is to eat a good diet. A high fat diet has been proven to cause eye damage. The very small capillaries that bring the much needed blood to the retina can become plugged, thus causing the retina injury.

We should always be careful to protect the eyes from something that might get into the eye, thus causing serious hurt. Keep the eyes away from sharp objects, and, when working with certain types of equipment, it is a good idea to wear safety goggles. In fact, eye protecting should be used when around any flying debris where there is a chance something could get into your eye. Sight is a precious gift God has given us and should be protected as much as possible.

24. How We Smell—If we wish to smell anything very strongly, we sniff or suddenly draw the air up through the nose. We do this to bring more air to the nerves of smell, which are placed at the upper part of the inside of the nose.

25. Smelling is a sort of feeling. The nerves of smell are so sensitive that they can discover things in the air which we cannot taste or see. We do not make so much use of the sense of smell as do the animals. Many persons lose the sense of smell altogether, maybe from a sickness or from working around strong chemicals. Smoking tobacco lessens our sense of smell also. Many animals can smell things a long distance away. Perhaps you have seen a dog put his nose up in the air and sniff. Our Creator has given some animals very good smelling abilities so that they can find food.

26. How We Taste—The tongue and the palate have very delicate nerves, by means of which we taste. We cannot taste with the whole of the tongue. The very tip of the tongue has only nerves of touch or feeling.

27. The use of the sense of taste is to give us pleasure and to tell us whether different substances could be healthful or injurious. Things which are poisonous and likely to make us sick almost always have an unpleasant taste, as well as an unpleasant odor. But remember, this is not always the case. We cannot trust our taste to determine whether something is poisonous or not.

28. **Bad Tastes**—People sometimes learn to like things which have a very unpleasant taste. Pepper, mustard, hot pepper sauce, and vinegar, alcohol, and tobacco are harmful substances of this sort. When used freely they injure the sense of taste, so that it cannot detect and enjoy fine and delicate flavors. These substances, as we have elsewhere learned, also do the stomach harm and injure the nerves and other parts of the body.

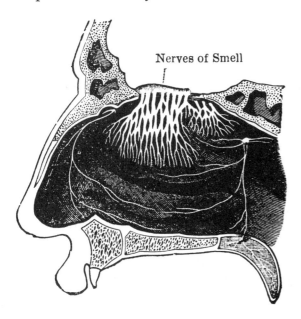

Nerves of Smell

INSIDE OF THE NOSE

29. **The Sense of Touch**—If you put your hand upon an object, you can tell whether it is hard or soft, smooth or rough, and can learn whether it is round or square, or of some other shape. You are able to do this by means of the nerves of touch, which are found in the skin in all parts of the body. If you wished to know how an object feels, would you touch it with the elbow, or the knee, or the cheek? You will say, No. You would feel of it with the hand, and would touch it with the ends of the fingers. You can feel objects better with the ends of the fingers because there are more nerves of touch in the part of the skin covering the ends of the fingers than in most other parts of the body.

30. The sense of touch is more delicate in the tip of the tongue than in any other part. This is because it is necessary to use the sense of touch in the tongue to assist the sense of taste in finding out whether things are good to eat or not. The sense of touch is also very useful to us in many other ways. We hardly know how useful it really is until we are deprived of some of our other senses, as sight or hearing. In a blind man the sense of touch often becomes surprisingly acute.

31. **Effects of Alcohol and Tobacco on the Special Senses**—All the special senses—hearing, seeing, smelling, tasting, feeling—depend upon the brain and nerves. Whatever does harm to the brain and nerves must injure the special senses also. We have learned how alcohol and tobacco, and all other narcotics and stimulants, injure and sometimes destroy the brain cells and their nerve branches, and so we can understand that a person who uses these poisonous substances will, by so doing, injure the delicate organs with which he hears, sees, smells, et cetera.

32. Persons who use tobacco and strong drink sometimes start to have poorer vision, because these poisons injure the nerves that give sight. The ears are frequently injured by the use of tobacco. Smoking cigarettes and snuff taking destroy the sense of smell. The poison of the tobacco paralyzes the nerves that give us taste so that they cannot detect flavors as well. This is why so many smokers like to use excessive amounts of salt, pepper, and other strong spices.

SUMMARY

1. God has given us five special senses—hearing, seeing, smelling, tasting, and feeling.

2. The ear is the organ of hearing. It has three parts, called the outer ear, the middle ear, and the inner ear. The inner ear contains the nerves that tell the brain what we hear.

3. The middle ear is separated from the outer ear by the eardrum. The eardrum is connected with the inner ear by a chain of bones.

4. Sounds cause the eardrum to vibrate. The ear bones convey the vibration from the eardrum to the nerves in the inner ear.

5. To keep the ears healthy, we must keep them clean and avoid putting things into them.

6. The eye is the organ of sight. The chief parts of the eye are the eyeball, the socket, and the eyelids.

7. In the eyeball are the pupil, the lens, the retina, and the nerves.

8. The eyeball is moved in various directions by six small muscles.

9. The eye is moistened by tears from the tear gland and the eye lids.

10. When we look at an object, the lens of the eye makes a picture on the retina, at the back part of the eyeball.

11. The nerves of smell are placed in the upper part of the inside of the nose.

12. Sometimes people lessen the sense of smell by smoking or by being around strong chemicals .

13. The nerves that taste are placed in the tongue and palate.

14. Many things which we think we taste we really do not taste, but smell or feel.

15. Usually, but not always, objects which have a pleasant taste are healthful, while those which have a bad taste are harmful.

16. Pepper, mustard, et cetera, as well as alcohol and tobacco, have an unpleasant taste and are not healthful. If we use them, we shall injure the nerves that taste, as well as other parts of the body.

17. We feel objects by means of the sense of touch.

18. The sense of touch is most acute at the tip of the tongue and the ends of the fingers.

Chapter 26

Alcohol

1. As we learned in the early part of our study of this subject, alcohol is produced by fermentation. It is afterwards separated from water and other substances by distillation. We will now learn a few more things about alcohol.

2. Alcohol Burns—If alcohol is placed in a lamp, it will burn much like kerosene oil. Indeed, it does not need a lamp to help it burn, as does oil. If a few drops of alcohol are placed upon a plate, it may be lighted with a match and will burn with a pale blue flame. Thus you see that alcohol is a combustible fluid.

3. The vapor of alcohol will burn also, and under some circumstances it will explode. On this account it is better not to try any experiments with it unless some older person is close by to direct you, so that no harm may be done. Alcohol is really a dangerous substance even though we do not take it as a drink.

4. An Interesting Experiment—We have told you that all fermented drinks contain alcohol. You will remember that wine, beer, and ale are fermented drinks. We know that these drinks contain alcohol because the chemist can separate the alcohol from the water and other substances, and thus learn just how much alcohol each contains.

5. If we should remove all the alcohol from wine, no one would care to drink it. The same is true of beer and cider. It is very easy to remove the alcohol by the simple process of heating. This is the way the chemist separated it. The heat drives the alcohol off with the steam. If the heating is continued long enough, all the alcohol will be driven off.

6. By a simple experiment, which your parents or your teacher can perform for you, it can be readily proven that different fermented drinks contain alcohol, and also that the alcohol may be driven off by heat. Place a basin half full of water upon the stove where it will soon boil. Put into a glass bottle enough beer or wine, so that when the bottle stands up in the basin the liquid in the bottle will be at about the same height as the water in the basin. Now place in the neck of the bottle a closely fitting cork in which there has been inserted a piece of the stem of a clay pipe or a small glass tube. Place the bottle in the basin. Watch carefully until the liquid in the bottle begins to boil. Now apply a lighted match to the end of the pipe-stem or glass tube. Perhaps you will observe nothing at first, but continue placing the match to the pipe-stem, and pretty soon you will notice a little blue flame burning at the end of the stem. It will go out often, but you can light it again. This is proof that alcohol is escaping from the liquid in the bottle. After the liquid has been boiling for some time, the flame goes out and cannot be relighted, because the alcohol has been all driven off.

7. The Alcohol Breath—You have doubtless heard that a person who is under the influence of liquor may be known by his breath. His breath smells of alcohol. This is because his lungs are trying to remove the alcohol from his blood as fast as possible, so as to prevent injury to the blood corpuscles and the tissues of the body. It is the vapor of alcohol mixed with his breath that causes the odor.

8. Making Alcohol—It may be that some of our young readers would like to find out for themselves that alcohol is really made by fermentation. This may be done by an easy experiment. You know that yeast will cause bread to "rise" or ferment. As we have elsewhere learned, a little alcohol is formed in the fermentation of bread, but is driven off by the heat of the oven in baking, so that we do not take any of it into our stomachs when we eat the bread. If we place a little baker's yeast in sweetened water, it will cause it to ferment and produce alcohol. To make alcohol, all we have to do is to place a little yeast and some sweetened water in a bottle and put it away in a warm place for a few hours until it has had time to ferment. You will know when fermentation has taken place by the great number of small bubbles which appear. When the liquid has fermented, you may prove that alcohol is present by means of the same experiment by which you found the alcohol in cider or wine.

9. Alcohol is made from the sweet juices of fruits by simply allowing them to ferment. Wine, as you know, is fermented grape juice. The strong alcoholic liquor obtained by distilling wine, cider, or any kind of fermented fruit juice, is known as brandy.

10. How Beer Is Made—Beer is made from grain of some sort. The grain is first moistened and kept in a warm place for a few days until it begins to sprout. The young plant needs sugar for its food; and so, while the grain is sprouting, much of the starch in the grain is changed into sugar. This, as you will remember, is the way in which the saliva acts upon starch. So far no harm has been done. Sprouted grain can be very good for you. Maybe you have eaten sprouted wheat bread. God intends that the sugar to be used as food for the little sproutlet; but the brewer wants it for another purpose, and he stops the growth of the plant by drying the grain in a hot room.

11. The next thing the brewer does is to grind the dried sprouted grain and soak it in water. The water dissolves out the sugar. Next he adds yeast to the sweet liquor and allows it to ferment, thus converting the sugar into alcohol. Potatoes are sometimes treated in a similar way. Doesn't it seem strange that men will go through all this work just to create a drink that brings harm to you?

12. By distilling beer or other fermented grains, called mash, a strong liquor known as whiskey is obtained. Sometimes juniper berries are distilled with the mash. The liquor obtained is them called gin. In the West Indies on the great sugar plantations, large quantities of liquor are made from the skimmings and cleanings of the vessels in which the sweet juice of the sugarcane is boiled down. These refuse matters are mixed with water and fermented, then distilled. This liquor is called rum.

13. Now you have learned enough about alcohol to know that it is not produced by plants in the same way that food is, but that it is the result of a sort of decay. Thus it is easily seen that it is not in God's plan for man use alcohol as a beverage. In making alcohol, good food is destroyed and made into a substance that is not fit for food, and which produces a great amount of sickness and destroys many lives. Do you not think it a pity that such great quantities of good corn and other grains should be wasted in this way when they might be employed for a useful purpose?

14. The Alcohol Family—Scientists tell us that there are several different kinds of alcohol. Naphtha is a strong-smelling liquid sometimes used by painters to thin their paint and make it dry quickly. It does not have the same odor as alcohol, but it looks and acts very much like it. It will burn as alcohol does. It kills animals and plants. It will make a person drunk if he takes a sufficient quantity of it. It is really a poison and can kill a person who drinks it. Indeed, it is very similar to alcohol in many ways.

15. There are also other kinds of alcohol. Amyl alcohol, or more commonly called fusel oil, is a deadly poison. A very small amount of this alcohol will make a person very drunk. Fusel oil used to be found in bad whiskey. All whiskey is bad, but some kinds are worse than others. Years ago people used to brew whiskey in their homes and would sometimes produce this type of alcohol, which would be very dangerous to drink. Sometimes people would lose their sight or even die There are still other kinds of alcohol, some of which are even worse than fusel oil. So you see this is a very bad family. Our Creator never intended for man to use alcohol in a way that would destroy the life He gave them.

16. Like most other bad families, this alcohol family has many bad relations. Ether and chloroform are relatives of alcohol. They are sometimes manufactured from alcohol. Although these substances at times have useful purposes, they are very poisonous and dangerous. Do you not think it will be very wise and prudent for you to have nothing to do with alcohol in any form, even wine, or beer, since it belongs to such a bad family and has so many bad relations?

17. Some persons think that they will suffer no harm if they take only wine or beer. This is a great mistake. A person may get drunk on any of these drinks if a sufficient amount be taken. Besides, young people who use wine or beer, rarely fail to become fond of stronger liquors. A great many men who have died drunkards began with beer. In fact, some men are beer drunkards.

18. "Bitters"—There are other liquids not called "drinks," which contain alcohol. "Bitters" usually contain more alcohol than is found in ale or wine, and sometimes more than in the strongest whiskey. "Jamaica ginger" is almost pure alcohol. Hence, it is often as harmful for a person to use these medicines freely, as to use alcoholic liquors in any other form.

19. Some Experiments—How many of you remember what you have learned in previous lessons about the poisonous effects of alcohol? Do people ever die at once from its effects? Only a short time ago a man made a bet that he could take five good-sized drinks of whiskey in just seconds. He dropped dead when he had swallowed the fourth glass. No one ever suffered such an effect from taking water or fruit juice or any other good food or drink.

20. A man once made an experiment by mistake. He was carrying some alcohol across a lawn. He accidentally spilled some upon the grass. The next day he found the grass as dead and brown as though it had been scorched by fire.

21. A well-known scientist once made a interesting experiment. He took a little plant with three healthy green leaves and shut it up under a glass jar where there was a teaspoonful of alcohol. The alcohol was in a dish by itself, so it did not touch the plant; but the vapor of the alcohol mixed with the air in the jar so that the plant had to breathe it. In less than half an hour he took the plant out. Its leaves were faded and somewhat shrivelled. The next morning it appeared to be dead. Do you suppose the odor of fruit juice or vegetable juice would affect a plant like that? Animals shut up in a confined area with alcohol will in time die in just the same way.

22. A Drunken Plant—How many of you

remember about an interesting plant that catches flies? Do you remember its name? What does the Venus's-flytrap do with the flies after it catches them? Do you say that it eats them? Really this is what it does, for it dissolves and absorbs them. In other words, it digests them. This is just what our stomachs do to the food we eat.

23. A few years ago a scientist thought that he would see what effect alcohol would have upon the digestion of a plant. So he put a fly-catching plant in a jar with some alcohol for just five minutes. The alcohol did not touch the plant, because the jar was only wet with the alcohol on the inside. When he took the plant out, he found that it could not catch flies, and that its digestion was spoiled, so that it could not even digest very tender bits of meat which were placed on its leaves. The plant was drunk.

24. Scientists have tried a great many experiments with various poisons, and found that the plants were affected in much the same way by ether and chloroform, and also by nicotine, the poisonous oil of tobacco. Sugar, milk, and other foods had no such effect. This does not look much as though alcohol would help digestion, does it?

25. **Effects of Alcohol on Digestion**—Dr. Roberts, a very eminent English scientist, made many experiments, many years ago, to ascertain positively about the effect of alcohol upon digestion. He concluded that alcohol, even in small doses, delays digestion. This is quite contrary to the belief of very many people, who suppose that wine, beer, or stronger liquors aid digestion. The use of alcohol in the form of beer or other alcoholic drinks is often a cause of serious disease of the stomach and other digestive organs.

26. **Effects of Alcohol on Animal Heat**—A large part of the food we eat is used in keeping our bodies warm. Most of the starch, sugar, and fat in our food serves the body as a sort of fuel. It is by this means that the body is kept always

at about the same temperature, which is just a little less than one hundred degrees—right around 98.6 degrees. This is why we need more food in very cold weather than in very warm weather.

27. When a person takes alcohol, it is found that instead of being made warmer by it, he is not so warm as before. He feels warmer, but if his temperature be measured by means of a thermometer placed in his mouth, it is found that he is really colder. The more alcohol a person takes, the colder he becomes. If alcohol were good food, would we expect this to be the case? It is probably true that the alcohol does make a little heat, but at the same time it causes us to lose much more heat than it makes. The outside of the body is not so warm as the inside. This is because the warm blood in the blood vessels of the skin is cooled more rapidly than the blood in the interior of the body. The effect of alcohol is to cause the blood vessels of the outside of the body to become much enlarged. This is why the face becomes flushed. A larger amount of warm blood is brought from the inside of the body to the outside, where it is cooled very rapidly; and thus the body loses heat, instead of gaining it, under the influence of alcohol. This is not true of any proper food substance.

28. **Alcohol in the Polar Regions**—Experience teaches the same thing as science respecting the effect of alcohol. Captain Ross, Dr. Kane, Captain Parry, Captain Hall, Lieutenant Greely, and many other famous explorers who have spent long months amid the ice and snow and intense cold of the countries near the North Pole, all say that alcohol does not warm a man when he is cold and does not keep him from getting cold. Indeed, alcohol is considered so dangerous in these cold regions that no Arctic explorer at the present time could be induced to use it. Years ago the Hudson Bay Company did not allow the men who worked for them to use any kind of alcoholic liquors. Alcohol is

a great deceiver, is it not? It makes a man think he is warmer, when he is really colder. Many men are frozen to death while drunk.

29. Alcohol in Hot Regions—Bruce and Stanley Livingstone, and all great African travellers, condemn the use of alcohol in that hot country as well as elsewhere.

30. Sunstroke—Do you know what sunstroke is? If you do not, your parents or teacher will tell you that persons exposed to the heat of the sun on a hot summer day are sometimes overcome by it. They become weak, giddy, or insensible, and sometimes even die. Scores of people are sometimes stricken down in a single day in some of our large cities. It may occur to you that if alcohol cools the body, it would be a good thing for a person to take to prevent or relieve an attack of sunstroke. On the contrary, it is found that those who use alcoholic drinks are much more liable to sunstroke than others. This is on account of the poisonous effects of the alcohol upon the nerves. No doctor would think of giving alcohol in any form to a man suffering with sunstroke.

31. Effects of Alcohol Upon the Tissues—Here are two interesting experiments which your teacher or parents can make for you.

Experiment 1. If you can get a piece of meat, perhaps a piece of beefsteak, place it in a saucer and cover it with alcohol. Put it away overnight. In the morning the beefsteak will be found to be shrunken, dried, and almost as tough as a piece of leather. This meat in the saucer is very similar to that of man. This shows the effect of alcohol upon the muscle tissue of the man who drinks.

Experiment 2. Break an egg into a half glassful of alcohol. Stir the egg and alcohol together for a few minutes. Soon you will see that the egg begins to harden and look just as though it had been boiled.

32. This is the effect of strong alcohol. The alcohol of alcoholic drinks has water and other things mixed with it, so that it does not act so quickly nor so severely as pure alcohol; but the effect is essentially the same in character. It is partly in this way that the brain, nerves, muscles, and other tissues of drinking men and women become diseased. Eminent physicians tell us that a large share of the unfortunate persons who are shut up in insane asylums are brought there by alcohol. Is it not a dreadful thing that one's mind should be thus ruined by a useless and harmful practice? God would have us to be healthy and happy.

A well-known Christian writer once said, "God does not require us to give up anything that it is for our best interest to retain. In all that He does, He has the well-being of His children in view. Would that all who have not chosen Christ realize that He has something vastly better for them than they seek for themselves. Man is doing the greatest injury and injustice to his own soul when he thinks and acts contrary to the will of God." God loves us and knows what is best for us. Let's place our trust in Him. And let us take good care of the wonderful house our Creator has given us to live in.

SUMMARY

1. Alcohol is produced by fermentation, and obtained by distillation. It will burn like kerosene oil and other combustible fluids.

2. The vapor of alcohol will burn and will sometimes explode.

3. Alcohol may be separated from beer and other fermented liquids by boiling.

4. Brandy is distilled from fermented fruit juice, whiskey and gin from beer or fermented grains, rum from fermented molasses.

5. Alcohol is the result of a sort of decay, and much good food is destroyed in producing it.

6. Besides ordinary alcohol, there are several other kinds. Naphtha and fusel oil are alcohols.

7. All the members of the alcohol family are poisons; all will burn, and all will intoxicate. The alcohol family have several bad relations, among which are carbolic acid, ether, and chloroform.

8. Beer and wine are harmful and dangerous, as well as strong liquors. "Bitters" often contain as much alcohol as the strongest liquors, and sometimes more.

9. Death can occur almost instantly from taking large quantities of strong liquors.

10. Alcohol will kill grass and other plants if poured upon them or about their roots.

11. Scientists have proved that the vapor of alcohol will kill plants, also that plants become intoxicated by breathing the vapor of alcohol.

12. Alcohol, even in small quantities, hinders digestion.

13. Alcohol causes the body to lose heat so rapidly that it becomes cooler instead of warmer.

14. The danger of freezing to death when exposed to extreme cold is greatly increased by taking alcohol.

15. Stanley and other African explorers say that it is dangerous to use alcoholic drinks in hot climates.

16. In very hot weather persons who use alcoholic drinks are more subject to sunstroke than those who do not.

17. A beefsteak soaked in alcohol becomes tough like leather. An egg placed in alcohol is hardened as though it had been boiled.

18. The effect of alcohol upon the brain, nerves, and other tissues of the body is much the same as upon the beefsteak and the egg.

Notes

Notes

Notes

Notes

Notes